Chesapeake Bay
Privateers

=== *in the* ===

Revolution

Chesapeake Bay Privateers

in the

Revolution

LEONARD SZALTIS

THE
History
PRESS

Published by The History Press
Charleston, SC
www.historypress.net

On the cover: Macgregor 1939. *Courtesy of the author.*

Unless otherwise noted, all images are public domain.

First published 2019

Manufactured in the United States

ISBN 9781467141789

Library of Congress Control Number: 2018963534

CONTENTS

FOREWORD

Author Leonard Szaltis has uncovered unique and interesting facts about the world of pirates, privateers and patriots, all of which are contained in this book. This truly insightful book sheds new light on the infamous and historical legends of privateers and examines the patriotic loyalties of the Revolutionary Eastern Shore. This work has identified a gap in Revolutionary War history—a gap that is about as big as the Atlantic Ocean.

The British fleet, the mightiest naval power in the world at that time, could carry soldiers and supplies in ample quantities to easily crush its rebellious colonial subjects. At the beginning of the conflict, there were not any Continental vessels to obstruct the English shipping, but by 1777, the colonists had thirty-four cruisers afloat. That was short-lived, because the British fleet had reduced that number to seven by 1782. However, even with just a small number of cruisers, the British vessels were not safe on the high seas while transiting their merchandise to the colonists.

As a quasi-legal, amateur civilian navy, privateers helped even the odds. Ship owners outfitted their own ships, and in doing so, they made a very large contribution to the independence of the United States. It has been estimated that the colonies had at least two thousand privately owned vessels involved in various aspects of the war. These ships were outfitted with eighteen thousand cannons and carried seventy thousand men who took part in the war. Because of the efforts of this private fleet, a total of 16 English warships and 2,980 British merchant vessels were captured. Based on their value, these prizes made nearly $50 million for ship owners and the volunteers who made the captures. Washington's hard-pressed army received much of the war booty, while King George III received nothing but grief.

Little is known about these privateers who combined patriotism with profit. This book introduces you to the privateers who stand tall among their liberty-loving countrymen as well as those who sought to defeat that cause.

Over two hundred printed references were used for this work, as were many original legal documents, journals and correspondence. Portraits and maps of the era are included to provide historical context to the real-life events that took place. These fragments have been gathered, sorted and compiled into *Chesapeake Bay Privateers in the Revolution*.

HILARY G. DERBY, PHD

ACKNOWLEDGEMENTS

There are many people who have helped with information for this book, including my grandmother, Ethel Bradshaw Dix Zavorski, my aunt Margaret Evans Marshall and cousin Jennings Evans, amongst other relatives and family friends native to the Eastern Shore.

Furthermore, several other scholars, historians, librarians and experts have been quintessential in this research. I would like to thank Thomas Ashby, Sons of the American Revolution genealogist, Capt. Zeally Moss Chapter, Illinois Society Sons of the American Revolution; Steve Callaway; Paul Chase, Colonel William Grayson Chapter, Virginia Society Sons of the American Revolution; Hilary G. Derby, PhD, Northumberland County, Virginia Historical Society; Sarah Kulp for photography; Andrew Risley, general collections library assistant, Newberry Library; Richard Sayre, director, Hewes Library, Monmouth College; Donald G. Shomette, naval historian and author; Christopher T. Smithson, Sons of the American Revolution genealogist, Maryland Society Sons of the American Revolution; Damon Talbot, special collections archivist, Maryland Historical Society; the research staff at the Library of Virginia; and John Van Ausdall for proofreading. While most of these individuals will not appear in the notes or bibliography, without their guidance, many of the original documents that were fundamental to create this historical record of early America would never have been discovered.

While researching this topic, it was found that members of the same family fought on both sides of the war. So, the question that came to mind was:

what would cause family members to fight against each other? For instance, a British privateer also fought for the Americans in the Maryland Militia. There was no prior research published on this subject that was readily accessible. This work seeks to provide evidence in order to understand the events that were occurring in the Chesapeake Bay during this time.

In order to provide factual, historical evidence, most of the sources have been quoted directly in their entirety. Considering the lack of evidence available in published media, it seemed necessary to provide all available information so other researchers could have access to it to conduct further examination. Therefore, this work contains exact quotations of historical government documents. This is the first time that most of these sources have been brought together in a published format. I encourage further research on the history of the Chesapeake Bay and the Eastern Shore of Maryland and Virginia during the Revolutionary War, and I hope that you find this work both informative and interesting.

INTRODUCTION

The perception of the American Revolution is that the American colonies were rebelling against oppressive British regulations. Since history is written by the victor, some people consider the war as an "us versus them" scenario. The Revolutionary War was not a simple two-sided war; there were many complexities that existed in the American colonies during this time. These additional facts portray varying perspectives of the Revolution and the convictions that were held by several different facets of colonial society. By July 1776, it was apparent that the colonial forces had gained enough momentum that John Murray (hereafter referred to as Lord Dunmore), governor of Virginia, and Governor Sir Robert Eden, 1st Baronet of Maryland, had both extricated themselves from the mainland of the colonies and ruled in exile upon British vessels in the Chesapeake Bay.[1] With few royal officials of the British government remaining in Virginia and Maryland, it became easy for colonial governments to establish themselves in both states. Councils of Safety and Correspondence were created at both the state and county levels and served as the "official" colonial government for the Patriots, but they were viewed as "extralegal entities" by those who were still loyal to the British Crown.

The Revolution did not have a simplistic idealism or altruism in the struggle between the British versus the Americans. The American Revolution has been considered by some as the first American Civil War. Not every colonist was a Patriot; some were quite content being under the rule of the British monarchy. Likewise, not everyone who fought against the colonial

Sir Robert Eden by Florence MacKubin after Charles Willson Peale, 1914. *Courtesy of the Collection of the Maryland State Archives.*

government was supportive of British rule. Many citizens who signed the Freemen of Maryland Oath—and even those who enlisted in the colonial militia—held strong Loyalist convictions. Besides differing political views, there were also economic and financial factors as well as divided religious ideologies and family and regional allegiances that applied to this struggle. These factors combined to bring a complicated understanding toward the motivations of American colonists during the time leading up to the Revolution. It can easily be concluded that the War for Independence was much more than a two-sided battle. "John Adams observed, the American Revolution was fought by one-third of the population against another third to benefit the remaining third."[2] This book can explain some of the reasons for such divisiveness amongst America's inhabitants.

A major concern in the minds of Eastern Shore colonists at the start of the Revolution was not the oppression of British rule but rather the uncertainty of a new government. Realistically, it took more than a decade for a new federal government to fully establish itself. Today, if someone said that the president was no longer in charge of the United States and that all of the laws of Congress could be disregarded and a new government is now in charge, the idea would sound ludicrous. That was exactly what the revolutionaries proclaimed to the nation's citizens. Those who refused to follow the new laws and pay their taxes could be fined, jailed or executed for treason.

A perfect example of this wariness was the "arbitrary and unprecedented Act of Tyranny" by Andrew Sprowle of Gosport, Norfolk County, Virginia.[3] He was a local merchant who founded and operated the Gosport Shipyard in 1767. That shipyard is now known as the Norfolk Naval Shipyard, which is the oldest operating shipyard for the U.S. Navy's Atlantic fleet. However, at the start of the American Revolution, Sprowle's shipyard harbored British ships during the winter months and openly operated under their flag. The Norfolk Council of Safety received knowledge of this detail and summoned Sprowle to appear in person. Earlier, another merchant by the name of John Schaw had been brought before the council, stripped naked, beaten and had nearly been tarred and feathered for supporting the British.[4] Knowing this prior punishment, Sprowle cunningly responded in writing and asked the council members what would they have done if two British men-of-war sailed into their harbor loaded with soldiers; he then cordially invited them aboard one of his ships if they wanted to continue the discussion.[5] The Council of Safety sent Sprowle a letter of understanding and stated that they would regretfully have to decline his invitation. The council might not have been as forgiving if they had known that not only had the British navy anchored at his shipyard, but Sprowle was personally hosting Lord Dunmore at his residence. The Royal Government of the Colony of Virginia was being operated from Sprowle's house with its navy practically parked in his backyard. Sprowle was able to maintain this charade until May 1776, when Lord Dunmore and the Royal Navy retreated and he was captured. His shipyard was confiscated by the Virginia Militia and used for its navy.

He was exiled to Gwynn's Island and died a few days later.[6] Andrew Sprowle was a Loyalist and cunning businessman who died in exile on an isolated island and was buried in an unmarked grave.

The only way for the Patriots to break from British rule and create a new democracy was to establish a legitimate government. The example of Andrew Sprowle clearly showed the ineffectiveness of some of the local councils of safety. If the governed people did not accept the governing body, it resulted in anarchy. This was the reality that the new American colonial government faced as they propelled themselves away from British imperialism and moved toward American independence.

One of the most tumultuous regions of the Revolution was the Chesapeake Bay. More specifically, it included the Delmarva (Delaware, Maryland and Virginia) Peninsula. This section of land (hereafter referred to as the Eastern Shore) was separated from the mainland of the continent by the Chesapeake Bay. This created several political and social divides between the "eastern shoremen" and the "mainlanders." For instance, on Smith Island, there were nineteen families noted living there but only five last names.[7] Often, the residents of the Eastern Shore relied on self-preservation and did not know about new laws and taxes that the state legislatures had passed until several weeks later. It can be obvious why there might have been distrust against the governments on the mainland when it came to the islanders and Eastern Shore residents.

In addition, the Chesapeake Bay was a prominent trading route for transporting goods; any disruption in this flow of trade was of vital concern to all the local residents who relied on this revenue. Concerns such as these fueled strong vehemence toward those on the opposing side of the rebellion. Because of the significant importance of this waterway, one of the major implementations instituted by the Maryland Convention was the Maryland State Navy. Though it was meager in number, it was essential in enforcing a steady flow of maritime traffic within the bay. The navy was under the control of the Council of Safety until the first state constitution was adopted on March 20, 1777, and thereafter, it was commanded directly by the governor of Maryland.[8]

This matter came to a crucial point in the fall of 1776, when the "salt riots" erupted in Dorchester and Talbot Counties in Maryland. Many staples, including salt, were being redirected for war efforts, which resulted in local families not being able to secure supplies for the winter. Residents of the Eastern Shore were primarily watermen and had only enough land to rely on subsistence farming for their family. Most of their commodities needed to be transported through the bay. Likewise, the major landholders took issue with unfair trade as well. Unlike the mainland, which profited in cash crops such as tobacco and cotton, the Eastern Shore primarily produced grain and other food staples. These food supplies were important to both sides of the war effort. Instead of profiting from their labor in the field, farmers were essentially being robbed of their crops in order to supply the troops. This disruption in trade was not only a matter of discontent amongst the residents of the Eastern Shore but also a clear matter of survival. They petitioned the Virginia Convention in 1776, stating:

> *Plantations have been ravaged, and our wives and children stripped almost to nakedness, our very bedchambers invaded, at the silent hour of midnight, by ruffians with drawn daggers and bayonets; our houses not only robbed of plate, specie, and everything valuable but wantonly reduced by fire to ashes.*[9]

Since the Chesapeake Bay was such a vital waterway for Loyalists and Patriots alike, it not only made it an important source for the trade of goods but also a main route for conveying information. The bay was used by the Continental Congress in Philadelphia to communicate with the Southern colonies and by the British to send messages to commanders in the field. In order to disrupt this flow of information and goods, both sides issued "letters of marque" to local sailors to become privateers. In essence, that meant they created "legally" licensed pirates to confiscate the opposition's ships, property and trade goods. Due to the fact that many sailors had their ordinary livelihoods disrupted, this created a lucrative opportunity in order to compensate them for their losses. "Privateering became the easiest method of annoying the enemy, and the profits held out to the undertakers made it a favorite form of maritime activity."[10] Both sides engaged in these types of subversive counterattacks, resulting in many Eastern Shore families colluding with the British. Early in the war, Colonel George Dashiell of Somerset County sent a dispatch to the governor of Maryland stating the effects of the devastating raids by privateers affecting the citizens of the Eastern Shore. In his depiction of the properties being plundered, Dashiell noted that the marauders were not British soldiers but were indeed known by the victims as inhabitants of the bay's islands.[11]

The letters of marque for American privateers were transferred from the records of the Continental Congress to the Library of Congress in 1903 and now reside in the National Archives.[12] Considering the lapse in time, the records are incomplete and provide only a survey of the ships in service during the war. A federal record of naval vessels and sailors during the Revolutionary War is not extant and relies heavily upon state muster rolls and payrolls from the states. Likewise, the records of British privateers are only preserved if their letters of marque managed to be returned to Great Britain. Overall, the collections of historical documents are spread across the National Archives, the Library of Congress, the British National Archives, the British Museum and the admiralty collection at the Public Records Office in Kew, London, and they will most likely never be entirely complete.

The Chesapeake Bay and the Eastern Shore were important regions in the outcome of the Revolutionary War. While major military battles were not of significant importance in this region, covert techniques helped both sides secure a strong supply chain and hinder the opposition's movements. In fact, the differing sides developed secret signals to indicate their true allegiance. For instance, Captain Joseph Wheland of Garden Island would raise and lower his mainsail three successive times. If the approaching vessel conducted the same act, he knew it was safe to sail the British Union Jack.

> *Here one should bear in mind that the confrontations between Loyalists and Patriots seldom escalated into armed confrontation. Loyalist activity usually consisted of passive or restrictive attempts to hamper the war-making power of the state.*[13]

The loyalties of the colonists may have had various subtle, complex reasons, but both sides had valid arguments to oppose the British or colonial governments.

The opposing forces engaged in a major conflict in the fall of 1782 featuring Commodore Zedekiah Whaley and Colonel John Cropper against Captain John Kidd and the British. This early-morning maritime engagement that occurred on November 30, 1782, became known as the "Battle of the Barges." "The 30 November Battle of the Barges, or properly called the Battle of Cager's Strait, was the bloodiest sea fight in which Maryland Naval forces engaged during the Revolution."[14] "They had no idea that the mortality rate on their flagship would soon be greater than in most other sea fights of the Revolution."[15] Lord Cornwallis had already surrendered at Yorktown in October 1781, and many colonists had thought that this brought an end to the war. However, it was not until the Treaty of Paris in September 1783 that the war would officially come to an end. More lives would be lost until the official conclusion of this conflict.

Charles Cornwallis, 1ˢᵗ Marquess Cornwallis, by Thomas Gainsborough, 1783. *Courtesy of the National Portrait Gallery, London.*

One of the major leaders of the Tory effort was Captain Joseph Wheland Jr. (Note: His name is spelled in various ways throughout historical documents, including Wheland, Wheeland, Wayland, etc.). Wheland served as the commander of the British privateer vessels and on occasion as the pilot for Lord Dunmore's fleet. Lord Dunmore was best known for being the governor of Virginia, but he issued many strategic commands for the

British vessels in the Chesapeake during the war. As the head of the British privateering effort, Wheland was considered to be the most-wanted fugitive by colonial officials in both Maryland and Virginia. The privateer was eventually captured but not before inflicting much damage to colonial ships and estates and confiscating requisite goods for the British troops. Dunmore was plagued by colonists who conducted their own acts of privateering against the Crown. Because of opposing viewpoints, this forced colonists to fight each other in a type of civil war.

Another interesting figure in the ensuing battle on the Chesapeake was Captain Stephen Mister, who was based out of Smith Island. The islanders, many of whom were from the same four or five families that founded the island, helped provide a safe haven for the pirates, and in return, the pirates did not harm the land or vessels at Smith Island.[16] That part of the island became known as Rogue's Point due to the fact that many of the privateers there were not actually issued letters of marque. Captain Winfred Evans explained the situation in a personal interview with Smith Island historian and author Francis Dize:

> *Sure they was pirates out here. Not in my granddaddy's lifetime; way back there in his daddy's time. I guess. Used to tell yarns about 'em. Why, Rhodes Point used to be Rogue's Point afore they changed it, you know.*[17]

The many inlets, marshes and waterways provided perfect concealment for the raiders of the islands and the Eastern Shore.

Mister's involvement was a family operation that significantly relied on his uncle, Marmaduke Mister, for his connections between the islanders and the Eastern Shore. While Stephen Mister seemed to do a vast amount of the confiscation of vessels and goods, he turned it over to his uncle to either forfeit the booty to the British or have him act as a middleman in order to fence the items for a profit. In all appearances, it seemed to be more of a family business venture than a crusade of political convictions.

Marmaduke and Stephen Mister were important characters in the Chesapeake privateer movement. Other members of the Mister family enlisted with American forces, including three nephews of Marmaduke Mister who enlisted in the Maryland Militia in 1780.[18] Ironically, Marmaduke Mister, after being accused of acts of piracy against the Patriot forces, also enlisted in the Maryland Militia.

A generation after the war, the Mister family still lived on Smith Island and nearby Deal Island, and the son of Marmaduke Mister, Severn Mister, and his sons continued to sail the bay. Furthermore, the family's Methodist religion compelled them to invite congregants to celebrate services in their own house with the local traveling pastor, Reverend Joshua Thomas. Even though Severn Mister had observant religious convictions, his faith would soon be tested by God when Reverend Thomas conveyed a premonition that he had received. This dream was more than a haunted warning—it was a premonition that affected the Mister family and brought the whole Chesapeake Bay community together in mourning.

This work neither delivers a detailed analysis of the Revolution nor depicts the history of one specific family. Instead, the intent of this book is to demonstrate the circumstances colonists faced in one local region during those bellicose times. It provides a series of vignettes, or short glimpses, into the real-life struggles that occurred during this tumult. Explicit examples describe grave encounters and suggest answers as to why many people in this area were divided in their loyalties and fought for opposing sides during the war. Finally, this work seeks to explore how members of the Mister family engaged in the American Revolution and how one family could represent both sides of the conflict. The purpose of this book is to increase knowledge about the history of the Chesapeake Bay and the Eastern Shore during the American Revolution.

Part One

LOYALIST SENTIMENTS
ON THE EASTERN SHORE

T he 1775 State Constitutional Convention formed the new colonial government of Maryland, but it was not viewed by everyone as having legitimate sovereignty until it eventually became part of the United States in 1781.[19] This new state government enacted the Treason Act, which created harsh punishments for anyone who defied the new government. The state government penalized professionals such as lawyers and doctors and even prohibited clergy and teachers from practicing if they were not considered loyal to the new, independent government.[20] At times, it seemed as if the rule of the British imperialistic government was less harsh than the new regulations imposed by the colonial government. The State of Maryland was extra-legal and therefore not recognized under international law—or by many of its own citizens. The new government confiscated the holdings of the former proprietary government and added those assets to the state treasury. The most imperative problem the fledgling government faced at this time was how to get the inhabitants to accept the legitimacy of the new government's authority.

During the early stages of the conflict, there was not one definition of a Loyalist. Those who were defined as Loyalists and Tories were not necessarily in support of the British monarchy, but anyone who opposed the new government could be labeled as such. There were many reasons why people supported either side of the war effort. Such reasons were not only political but also social, religious and economic in nature. Barry Paige Neville, assistant professor of history at Eastern Shore Community College, identified three distinct causes for why some members of the Eastern Shore chose to support the Loyalist side of the effort. The actual definition of a Loyalist or Tory was a person who was in full support of British rule, and there were citizens on the Eastern Shore who were loyal to the Crown. Secondly, there were some Americans who opposed the new policies of the state and federal government. Finally, based on Neville's conclusions, there were religious factions that opposed the war effort. The Anglican Church had obligatory loyalty to the British monarch, and other conservative Christian groups altogether opposed war.

In addition to those causes, there were other reasons why people on the Eastern Shore sided with the British. For instance, many of the families who inhabited the area dated back several generations and were interrelated to each other, with many of them being direct descendants of British colonists. Furthermore, there were significant concerns among these simple families whose lives were being economically affected by loss of revenue in fishing as well as the seizure of farm goods taken from them in order to support the American and British forces. Finally, some individuals saw an easy way to make a profit by becoming privateers for either side of the war effort. Some such individuals included Joseph Wheland Jr. and his mates Marmaduke and Stephen Mister. Wheland himself was arrested numerous times, as was Stephen Mister. Their offenses were committed against friend and foe alike, but the spoils were sent to Marmaduke Mister to make a profit. These were all reasons why many people of the Eastern Shore were linked to Loyalist movements.

In a bit of hypocrisy, the new state government retained the property qualifications for voters and elected officials. One cause for the creation of a new government was the British government's restriction of the rights of the colonists, yet the new government maintained the same qualifications: "All freemen over the age of twenty-one possessing a minimum of fifty acres of land or owning property worth at least £40 sterling could elect delegates to represent them in Annapolis."[21] The fishermen and farmers of the Eastern Shore had been waiting for equal suffrage but found themselves in the same condition as they were in under British rule. The requirements to be elected were even higher. One had to possess £500 of real property to serve as a delegate, and to serve on the council, one had to be worth £1,500.[22] For example, in Kent County, Maryland, that meant that out of 3,500 free white males, only 74 could meet the voting qualifications.[23] It is easy to understand why many people on the Eastern Shore grew discontented with the colonial government since they were unable to contend with large cities such as Annapolis or Baltimore.

The new government that was formed had no place for a common person. Neville gives quite a summation of America's Revolution:

The gentry's efforts to restrict the franchise and limit office holding illustrates a phenomenon peculiar to the American Revolution. In contrast to Marx's dialectic, where the oppressed proletariat led the revolution, or the middle class in the French Revolution, the American Revolution was shaped primarily by the gentry.[24]

Additionally, while there was not a formal conscription or draft for soldiers, any male between the ages of eighteen and fifty was expected to enlist or provide service to the war effort. Those who did not volunteer in the military or government could be fined between two and ten pounds.[25] Many men who did not have a conviction for the independent colonies enlisted out of fear of retribution from the new government. One such case occurred in 1775 in Frederick County, Maryland, when noncommissioned colonial officer Robert Gassaway stepped out of formation and announced to the muster of soldiers, "It was better for the poor people to lay down their arms and pay the duties and taxes levied by the King and Parliament than to be brought into slavery and to be ordered about as they were."[26]

In 1777, Isaac Atkinson, a landowner in Somerset County, Maryland, tried to raise a rebellion.[27] During a mustering of troops, he started recruiting the militia's soldiers and convinced them to side with the British. He stated that his intentions were to "oppose the Congress and Convention, for that he did not like any of the proceedings, or anything they had done."[28] He was arrested and brought before the court to be tried for treason. When Atkinson was brought for arraignment to the Somerset County courthouse, he was escorted by fifty of his followers, and the judge had no choice other than to drop the charges and release him. During the period of 1777–78, it is estimated that there were at least three hundred Tory forces in Somerset and Worcester Counties.[29]

In two instances, justices of the peace made public statements in opposition to the new government. First, James Clarke of Baltimore made an insinuation that if people just kept their mouths shut they would soon get back the fines paid for not mustering in the local militia, and he further went on to declare that he would never take up arms for the defense of America.[30] Like most dissidents of the new government, if one retracted his statement or apologized and signed an oath of loyalty, the sentence was minute. However, another judge, Francis Saunderson, who actually

Portrait of William Paca by Charles Willson Peale, 1822. *Courtesy of the Collection of the Maryland State Archives.*

was a member of the Committee of Observation, did not get by with such a light sentencing. He made "sundry expressions which appeared to us of such dangerous tendency" that they had the militia escort him for his sentencing—not because of his chance of escape but rather for his protection from the populace.[31] Obviously, freedom of speech did not exist at the time, and the convention fined Saunderson £1,000 for remarks of discouragement toward American freedom.[32]

Financially, the colonists were being pressed hard by the new government to pay taxes in order to support the war effort. Furthermore, any Continental currency had little or no backing and consisted of nothing more than promissory notes. The local militia was ordered to assist county sheriffs in collecting taxes from the residents of the Eastern Shore. In a sense of irony, the soldiers were basically ordered to go out and collect their own pay. In 1781, the payment of taxes from Somerset County, Maryland, became so resistive that on February 3, one hundred militiamen were sent from Dorchester County into Somerset to enforce the collection of taxes.[33] Maryland governor William Paca further explained the financial hardships of the colonists in a correspondence he sent to the Maryland State Council on February 19, 1783:

> *It has, for some Time past, been the Wisdom and Policy, of our General Assembly to effect, if possible, a Restoration of public Credit; thoroughly persuaded that no Country is able to prosecute an expensive War by an*

immediate and prompt Supply of Money from the Pockets of its People…
The Public Creditors are thus entitled to their interest.[34]

The governor warned the council that the public feared that their faith had been violated, and that if action was not taken, they might not follow the legislature of the new government.[35]

More importantly, the Eastern Shore was being robbed of many commodities on which they relied. Both sides of the war effort needed goods to support the troops, and the British and Loyalist privateers were not only confiscating and looting the houses and livestock of Eastern Shore residents but were also burning their houses and barns and indenturing slaves into the service of the British. Because the British forces were blockading the importation of many essential goods, this meant the colonial forces confiscated much of their produce from local farmers on the Eastern Shore. This, in turn, created animosity toward the new government. The following map portrays the deployment of the French and British fleets around the opening of the Chesapeake Bay. The left side of the map depicts troop movements around Yorktown, while above the legend on the right, it shows the ship *le Terrible*, which sank, engulfed in flames.

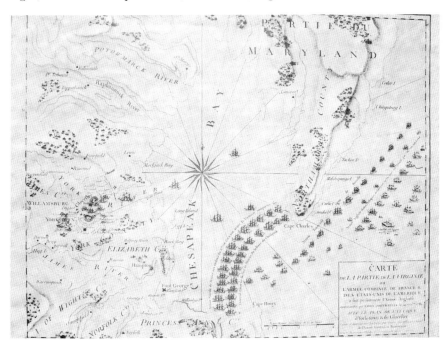

Map of part of Virginia with the combined army of France and the United States of America that captured the British army commanded by Lord Cornwallis on October 19, 1781, with the plan of the Yorktown and Gloucester attack (Paris 1781). *Courtesy of the author.*

State governments would confiscate livestock and other commodities from residents without reimbursement. In one such incident in September 1781, Virginia governor Thomas Nelson Jr. declared the state treasury depleted and issued a warrant to Colonel John Cropper to confiscate the alcoholic spirits from the Eastern Shore to supply the Virginia Militia. An example of the goods being used by the Continental army in 1780 included 5,200,000 pounds of beef; 48,000 barrels of flour; 4,000 bushels of salt; 17,000 gallons of rum; 56,162 bushels of corn; 5,500 bushels of pork; 200 tons of hay; and 1,000 hogshead's-worth of tobacco.[36] In return, farmers and landowners were being paid with promissory notes and declining Continental currency. These notes were traded at less than face value—if they were accepted as payment at all. Even Maryland's traditional cash crop, tobacco, was having difficulty being traded because the British blockade impeded overseas sales.[37] To his best ability, any time Cropper had to obtain various goods and articles, he actually tried to pay out of his own estate, which left him a relatively poor man by the end of the war.

In drastic contrast, almost in a sense of irony, Governor Paca, in his correspondence to the Maryland State Council, actually blamed the American colonists for not supporting the state:

> *In Cases where the Honor of the General Assembly is at Stake, or Public Faith pledged for a punctual Performance of an Engagement, or where Supplies are granted for the Defence and Protection of the State; a Sale should be made, with all possible Expedition. It is miserable financing to wait for a rising Market to get an additional Price… in the Mean Time, the Honor of the State is sacrificed, its Faith Violated, its Commerce interrupted, its Citizens plundered by the Enemy and drove from their Habitations, their Houses burnt, and Farms desolated, and Property destroyed and lost, to the Amount of Thousands; while the Public, on the Chance of a rising Market, are aiming to get so many Shillings and Sixpences.*[38]

Governor Paca was infuriated with the cavalier attitude of Maryland's residents and their opportunistic greed. Such an attitude also fueled the privateer movement that was prominent in the Chesapeake Bay during the Revolutionary War.

The most important good that was in jeopardy during this time was salt, because in the time before refrigeration, salt was essential for the preservation of meat. The British cut off the supply chain of salt imported from the Caribbean. Additionally, the Continental army obtained most of

Thomas Nelson Jr. by Henry Bryan Hall, etched by H.B. Hall, from a drawing in the collection of Dr. T[homas] A[ddis] Emmet, 1870.

their salt supplies from this region in order to supply the American forces. Only the richest citizens could afford to obtain salt. This created the salt riots in the fall of 1776 in Dorchester and Talbot Counties in Maryland, which Dorchester reported, "the want for the absolute necessities of life is so great that many families for months past have not had a spoonful of salt."[39] There were multiple raids upon wealthy landowners who were hoarding all of the salt. One such raid was conducted by Richard Andrew upon the estate of James Murray of Hunting Creek in Dorchester County. The crowd took fourteen and a half bushels of salt. In due respect, Andrew offered to pay Mrs. Murray for the salt taken, but she refused. Andrew, being an honest man, left fourteen dollars and fifty cents sitting on the table.

Two months later, Jeremiah Colston led a raid on the estate of James Chamberlaine, who was away serving in the militia at the time. The crowd forced the caretaker to open the storeroom, and each of the seventeen men took a bushel of salt. Chamberlaine and the militia managed to capture Colston shortly thereafter and took him before the court. At the trial, John Gibson, a member of the Committee of Observation, chastised Chamberlaine and *not* Colston for having hoarded salt when several of his Patriots needed it so desperately:

> *I need not remind you of these distressing times…no violence has occurred and [I] Hope that you'll not think them men of seditious principles who might be desirous of stirring up party factions. They are not such. I know several of the leading men to be men of reputation…* [and] *good moral character.*[40]

Due to the committeeman's testimony as a character witness, Colston and the other raiders received only a mild punishment for their action.

Commerce was not the only culprit to fuel the Eastern Shore skirmishes; religion factored into this war as well. Barry Paige Neville made a clear and concise observation when he stated, "It has always been infinitely easier for a revolutionary group to change the existing political system than to legislate the religious beliefs of the people."[41] One of the requirements for all Anglican clergymen was to make an oath of allegiance to the head of the Church of England, who was the monarch of Great Britain. This requirement was a basic tenet of ordination into the Anglican priesthood. When the Maryland state government required its inhabitants to take an oath of allegiance to the state and not the Crown, it essentially forced priests to renounce their religious vows. Father John Bowie, the minister of St. Martin's Parish in Worcester, was arrested in 1777 and imprisoned at Annapolis when he failed to pledge the state's loyalty oath and declared that he would rather "suffer his right arm to be cut off, and wished if he took it his tongue might cling to the roof of his mouth and never come loose."[42] This not only affected the priesthood, but parishioners had the same dilemma and had to make the choice between supporting liberty or the head of the Church of England.

Those who did not take the state oath of loyalty were deemed traitors in the eyes of the state. In order to appease the new state government,

Anglican bishops William White and Samuel Seabury supported new legislation. The Vestry Act, passed by the Maryland Council in 1779, resulted in church authority being transferred from the Anglican Church to the vestry of individual parishes. While the authority may have been transferred, the allegiance of the priests and parishioners may not have been. Of the thirty Anglican priests on the Eastern Shore in 1776, only fifteen were still residing there by 1780, and this was reduced to only two by 1784.[43] White went on to become the first presiding bishop of the Episcopal Church in the United States and also served as the second chaplain for the U.S. Senate.

Bishop William White by Gilbert Stuart, 1795. Bequest of William White. *Courtesy of the Pennsylvania Academy of the Fine Arts, Philadelphia.*

Another religious group that received misgivings for their beliefs was the Methodist Communion. Methodism grew in popularity along the Eastern Shore and is still the leading denomination present today. Methodism was founded by John Wesley and is technically a derivative of the Episcopal (Anglican) church. Therefore, there was still a close connection to the British monarchy, though the clergy were not bound by the same vows as Anglican priests. Additionally, one major tenet of the faith was to not bear arms. Therefore, most members objected to serving in the state militia. As a result, the state viewed these "contentious objectors" as sympathizers to the Loyalist cause.

One notable case was that of minister Freeborn Garrettson, who was born in Hartford County, Maryland, in 1752.[44] The Maryland oath of loyalty not only required obedience to the state but also to take up arms, if necessary, in its defense. As a pacifist Methodist, Garrettson refused to take the Maryland oath and stated, "I want in all things to keep a conscience void of offense, to walk the safest way, and to do all the good I can in bringing sinners to God."[45] Garrettson began his religious career when he was just nine years old, when he heard a voice say, "Ask and it shall be given you." He prayed to the Lord to make him a saint, and he heard the response, "A saint is one who is wholly given up to God. 'The voice is so real as if someone is talking to me face to face.'"[46] Garrettson's refusal to take an oath of loyalty brought the accusation of treason. On June 24, 1778, in Chestertown, Maryland, Garrettson was arrested and taken to Judge John Brown for his treason against the newly formed country.[47] While in prison, Garrettson held religious services for crowds gathered outside his cell's window. When Garrettson was brought before Brown, the latter asked him to make his plea. Garrettson informed Brown of the judge's imminent damnation and "sentenced" *him* to read his scriptures.[48] Taken aback, the judge dropped all charges and saw that he was truly looking into the face of a man of God. Garrettson was later kidnapped in the middle of the night, and the mob carried him off to be hanged; as they approached the lynching tree, it was struck by lightning, and the crowd dispersed.[49] He eventually capitulated and took the Delaware Oath of Allegiance, which did not contain a clause of taking up arms against the enemy.

Another example was that of Reverend John Patterson. He was arrested by the Patriots in 1775 and spent six months in jail before he managed to elude his captors and escape; he later went on to serve as a chaplain for the Philadelphia Loyalist Regiment.[50] Neville contends that if the states were observant toward religious tolerance, there might have been a more

Freeborn Garrettson by J. Thomson. *Courtesy of the United Methodist General Commission on Archives and History.*

sympathetic cause on the Eastern Shore. Since the King of England was the head of the church, the new government had difficulty delineating the two institutions. For this reason, the very first clause in the Bill of Rights dictates the concept of a separation of church and state.

A final example was the case against Reverend John Lyons of St. George Parish in Accomack County, Virginia. The reverend was a staunch Loyalist and publicly preached against the rebellion. It was also known that at least on one occasion, he had provided his own personal vessel to ship supplies to the British at Portsmouth. The pastor was such an influential person in the community that most parishioners were afraid to make statements against him. In fact, many citizens signed a petition for the court to rule in favor of acquitting the minister. On September 30, 1781, Colonel John Cropper of the Virginia Militia sent Lyons to Richmond along with the written demand for clemency for the cleric. Colonel Cropper wrote in a personal letter to the governor that the pastor needed "to settle his private business in this County....Since his confinement...he has often expressed to me his desire & intention of becoming a good citizen shou'd he be indulged with any degree of liberty."[51]

For the most part, the new colonial government handed down lenient punishments to those offenders who resisted the new government. There were a couple of cases that were much more severe and were intended to serve as an example to other Loyalists along the Eastern Shore. One such case occurred in Talbot County, Maryland, in September 1778 in the General Court of the Eastern Shore during the trial of John Tims, who was on trial for treason against the newly formed government. In an unusually harsh sentence, Judge Hanson ordered that Tims:

> *Be drawn to the place of execution and there hanged by the neck and cut down alive and that his entrails be taken out and burned before his face and his head cut off and his body divided into four quarters and his head and quarters disposed of at the pleasure of the state.*[52]

In a dreadful sense of hypocrisy, this was the typical punishment given by the British government in cases of treason. The wife of the accused had Sheriff William Wright of Queen Anne's County deliver a letter to Governor Thomas Johnson stating that the soon-to-be widow would be left alone with two children at home and did not have any way to provide for herself.[53] Additionally, the sheriff also testified that the radical punishment for such a miniscule criminal was not justified due to the fact that the leaders of the Tory movement were the ones the government should be seeking to incarcerate. In March 1779, the Maryland Council agreed with the sheriff and overruled the court's decision. Judge Hanson would later have his vengeance when three traitors were hanged in

Thomas Johnson Jr. by Charles Willson Peale, 1824. *Courtesy of the Collection of the Maryland State Archives.*

Frederick, Maryland, but Governor Johnson forbade the drawing and quartering of the individuals.[54]

Overall, it defaulted for the colonists to respect the legitimacy of the new national and state governments. Basically, every resident needed to evaluate whether or not his or her life would be better under British rule or if a new government would even be functional. The credibility of Maryland's new government, considering it was not a legal state, relied on "its ability to control the state's population, either by force or by persuading Maryland residents that it was the legal heir-apparent to the old governmental system."[55]

PART TWO

THE PATH TO PRIVATEERS
IN THE CHESAPEAKE BAY

In 1777, Loyalist activities on the Eastern Shore wreaked havoc upon the financial stability of the Continental forces. The American forces' supplies and money reached a critically low point. The Chesapeake Bay was a vital route for the colonists to send communiques from Philadelphia to all of the Southern colonies. Likewise, the British relied on the bay in order to provide their troops with a sustainable source of food. At this time, the British occupied Smith Island, Tilghman Island and Hoopers Island, while raiding parties of pirates and marauders were burning estates and farms across the region.[56] This not only inflicted a financial blow to the colonists but placed a demand for goods to supply both sides of the war.

On March 3, 1777, Captain Stewart and Captain James Campbell of Maryland's navy were ordered by Brigadier General William Smallwood to catch the Loyalist pirates Hamilton Callalo and Thomas Moore, who were said to be harboring at Smith Island.[57] The captains used the ruse of flying under British colors, but when Campbell sent Stewart ashore, he found that the picaroons had already escaped. Unfortunately, within two hours, Callalo had returned and rendezvoused with the British. Campbell was so infuriated that he returned and declared Smith Island a "place of reception of deserters and escaping prisoners," and he threatened that any person would hang who was found giving aid to the enemy.[58] Smallwood was convinced that the two would be captured, so he decided to wait before he sent the other prisoners that he had captured to Annapolis.

Campbell continued his pursuit of these elusive criminals for the next several days. On March 7, 1777, Captain Campbell spotted Callalo's ship, the *Phenix* [*sic*], around the area of Tangier Straits; however, everyone managed to escape into the marshes except for Levin Evans.[59] General Smallwood wrote to Campbell that Evans was a well-known privateer in the bay, so Campbell delivered him to Captain N. Smith. Apparently, Smallwood had been referring to a different Evans, and Campbell had apprehended the wrong man.

This is what the Maryland Council of Safety said on March 26, 1777, regarding the incident with Levin Evans:

> *Levin Evans of Somerset County, who was seized by James Campbell on the Lower Islands of this State within the forty days allowed by the Proclamation issued by the General Assembly, prayed for his release, and that he might be permitted to take the oath of fidelity to this State, and the said Levin Evans alleges that he was seized by mistake instead of one Richard Evans…*

> *The said Levin Evans, after his being discharged as aforesaid voluntarily took the said oath of Fidelity before the Governor and Council.*[60]

Some of these pirates received official letters of marque from the Crown and enjoyed the financial benefits of supplying the British with confiscated goods. In the spring of 1778, the Maryland state government tried a different maneuver and sent attorney Luther Martin to the Eastern Shore to examine the effects of the pirates.[61] Martin engaged with the sheriff of Somerset County to set about apprehending the privateer fleet. His response to the state government demonstrated the degree of Loyalist influence in the region:

> *The disaffected inhabitants of* [Somerset] *County… have arrived to so daring a height of insolence and Villainy that there appears but very little Security for [the] lives or property of any person who from political or other reasons are obnoxious to them… The Sheriff does not dare to go [to] Annemessex [River] to summon witnesses against the criminals who await their trial at the Special Court, and some of the most material witnesses live in that neighborhood… Several Boats with tobacco, Wheat Flower [sic] etc. have been taken away from Pocomoke, Jones Creek, [and] Wicomico…recently.*[62]

Luther Martin by Albert Rosenthal, 1905. *Courtesy of Historical and Special Collections, Harvard Law School Library Archives.*

The report from Martin was received by Governor Thomas Johnson of Maryland, who in turn implored the state legislature to offer stricter penalties in order to enforce the new state government on the Eastern Shore. The governor asked the state government to impose martial law in Somerset County with the possibility of executions and ordered 150 militiamen into the area.[63] Martin would later become the longest-serving attorney general for Maryland, remaining in office for twenty-eight consecutive years.[64] He is best known for acting as a defense attorney for Aaron Burr after Thomas Jefferson accused him of treason in 1807 for supposedly trying to make the Louisiana Purchase a new country, for which Burr was acquitted.

By early 1778, the Loyalists had managed to organize a force of over three hundred men in Somerset and Worcester Counties in Maryland. Additionally, the British warship the *Roebuck* gave them three pieces of artillery. The Loyalist forces destroyed the ammunition and powder magazine for the Somerset County Militia. The Maryland government was facing a dire situation in which they could lose the Eastern Shore to Loyalist forces. The state ordered Colonel Henry Hooper to take command of the Maryland Militia in Salisbury and ordered the state's navy, the *Enterprise*, the *Defense* and the *Dolphin* to assist in the elimination of Tory raids. Hooper sought additional resources from the Maryland state government, which

William Smallwood (1732–1792) from life by Charles Willson Peale, 1781–82. *Courtesy of the Collection of the Maryland State Archives.*

petitioned Congress to send the Continental Army. On February 1, 1778, Congress directed General William Smallwood to lead a Virginian infantry unit to proceed into Maryland to provide reinforcements.[65] They also authorized Maryland to raise a number of new troops and artillery in order to confirm the allegiance of its residents:

> *The deployment of troops from another state demonstrated a lack of trust in using local militias to suppress Toryism. And with good reason: desertion was rampant, local units often refused to leave their own counties to serve, and those that did often looted the surrounding countryside.*[66]

Portrait of John Murray, 4th Earl of Dunmore (1730–1809) by Sir Joshua Reynolds, 1765. Purchased in 1992 with contributions from the Art Fund and the National Heritage Memorial Fund. *Courtesy of the National Galleries of Scotland.*

In opposition, William Barkley Townshend, a wealthy landowner in Worcester County, Maryland, petitioned the British governor, Lord John Dunmore, to send British troops to fight the rebels. Townshend started gathering weapons and munitions, which aroused the suspicion of the local Council of Safety. The state government started to make inquiries, and in fear, Townshend fled to Virginia. The local government indicted him "in absentia" and confiscated all of his property, including the stockpiled arms and ammunition.[67] Upon his return, Townshend received only a mild fine, but it is not known if his confiscated property was ever returned.

Lord Dunmore was most generally noted as the British governor of the Colony of Virginia, but many Loyalists of the period praised his prowess as a military commander. That is one reason why he was so influential toward the attempts of the British to control the Chesapeake Bay. The disapproval of Dunmore had reached an all-time high in the early 1770s, when he conducted a war with the Shawnee Native Americans. It has been speculated that he colluded with the Shawnee tribe in order to engage the Virginia Militia to deflect attention away from the growing tensions between the British and the colonists. This not only stretched the militia's forces but also increased taxes to support "Dunmore's War," as it came to be known. In any regard, Dunmore did not have any serious respect for the colonial governmental institutions or colonial militias. Like many other British politicians and military commanders, he did not take the Patriot movement seriously—or at least he underestimated its effectiveness.

While the militias were fighting on the Eastern Shore, there was a separate, even more distinct battle occurring on the waters of the Chesapeake Bay. The privateer fleet was officially sanctioned to attack and confiscate the property of the enemy. In total Congress issued 1,697 letters of marque for private citizens to engage the British, and that does not include almost 200 letters granted by the colonies of Maryland and Virginia.[68] It is estimated that approximately seventy thousand men served aboard American privateering vessels in the colonies. By comparison, the Continental navy had approximately three thousand men and fifty-three ships, including thirteen frigates, but never had more than eight frigates sailing at any given time.[69] This demonstrates the importance and significance of privateers during the Revolution.

PART THREE

JOSEPH WHELAND

he most famous of the Loyalist sea captains ('pirates' in the eyes of the state government) was Joseph Whaland."[70] (Note: Hereafter, the captain shall be referred to as "Wheland" unless a variation is directly quoted.) Wheland was described as a "tall, slim, gallows looking fellow."[71] The captain was originally from Garden Island, and his crew was based out of Tangier Island, which is located in the Chesapeake Bay directly south of the Maryland-Virginia border.[72] Wheland became a close associate of British commander Lord Dunmore in 1776 and helped transport goods up the Potomac River for the British. By June 1776, he served as a pilot for Dunmore's ships through the bay and its tributaries.[73] In return, he was given free rein to oversee his own fleet of vessels to raid the Eastern Shore.

Wheland was in command of the man-of-war *Tender* when he witnessed a sailor from the Eastern Shore towing confiscated wrecks to scrap salvageable parts and goods. (Note: The term "tender" refers to a transport vessel or a supporting cargo ship for a larger warship. Since the actual vessel's name is not identified, it shall be referred to as *Tender*.) The next day, Wheland seized the main vessel and sailed off with her cargo. The salvager, Nathan Linton, went to Captain Matthew Squire aboard the British vessel the *Otter* and complained that he had not been recompensed for the goods confiscated by Wheland.[74] The captain invited Linton aboard his ship to discuss the reimbursement of his losses. In an offer of kindness, he gave Linton a gallon of rum, some pork and five barrels of oil; in the meantime, while Captain Squire was entertaining this guest aboard his ship, his men confiscated the remaining cargo of rum and iron from the other wrecks in Linton's possession.[75] In this situation, it might have been better if Linton had cut his losses.

The primary reason why Wheland was granted this command was to conduct military raids against the Patriots to inhibit their infrastructure and the stability of their government. Like some pirates of the Revolution, Wheland turned to looting and sought to satisfy personal vendettas. On June 25, 1776, Wheland commanded two ten-gun sloops and a schooner and sailed to Hopkins Island, where he confiscated over sixty cattle.[76] In the following days, Wheland and his associates carried out a number of raids on the Eastern Shore. In the middle of the night, they attacked William Roberts of the Dames' Quarter District of Somerset County, Maryland, and bound him hand and foot and dragged him and his slaves onboard. Later, on June 30, they set fire to the home of Samuel McChester at Nanticoke Point as another act of hostility.[77] Wheland soon became known to colonial officials as one of the most notorious and mischievous brigands upon the bay.

In the previous months, Wheland and his crew had disrupted commerce throughout the Chesapeake Bay, primarily in the region of Hooper's Strait, which is located between Hoopers and Bloodsworth Islands. Wheland went on to confiscate a sloop from John White, which he was planning to use "to guard the Islands and keep the Shirt Men [Virginia militiamen] from going on to abuse the inhabitants."[78] Eventually, in July 1776, he was arrested for torching and destroying the sloop at Vienna in the Nanticoke River, though he maintained he was innocent.[79]

The following descriptions go into great detail to explain that event. On July 15, Wheland and his mate, Marmaduke Mister, encountered a vessel off Smith Island.[80] It was the vessel of Captains Joseph Mariman and Moses Yell that had departed the Honga River and was headed for the Potomac when they spotted the British and sought refuge at Smith Island.[81] The pirates boarded the vessel of Master Yell and immediately began questioning the loyalty of Yell and Mariman. Wheland asked, "Who was right? King or Shirtmen?" Yell replied, "The Americans."[82] Wheland informed Yell that he had orders to destroy any vessel that was not of use to the British fleet. The picaroons took forty schillings from the vessel plus all of the crews' clothing minus that which was left upon their backs. The prisoners were transferred to the *Tender*, and Marmaduke Mister was put in place to guard them.

During the internment, Mister once again questioned Yell's allegiance:

The prisoner answered diplomatically that "he was a Friend to every person that behav'd well."
"In the King's name," commanded Mister, "tell the Truth."
"I was born in this country and have a right to defend liberty."
"What these damned rebels call liberty," sneered the guard, "I call slavery, and so the people will find it." [83]

The following are official depositions of this event that led to his downfall and are reproduced in their entirety, including grammatical and spelling errors.

MARIMAN'S DEPOSITION

July 27 1776
Joseph Mariman being sworn on the Holy Evangels of Almighty God deposeth and sayeth that about the 15th day of this Instant he with Moses Yell left the mouth of Hungar River in a Vessel bound to Potomac loaded with Plank and Tar, but being in a hard gale and a large swell they were obliged to put back, but on their attempting to put back the tide headed them, they afterwards hove about and stood for the mouth of the Potomack again, and about day break they espied Lord Dunmore's fleet at the distance of about a mile, they then hove about and stood for Smyth's Islands and there came to anchor they stayed there about two or three hours, the wind moderated, the Deponent went ashore to Smyths Island in order to buy some fish and to seek for a Canoe he had lost the night before, and to enquire if there was no inlet there to make a better Harbour, and to get some fire to cook with. Before he got ashore he saw two men in a Canoe approaching him, which he understood afterwards was Joseph Wheeland Jun' and one Lazarus, a Mulatto, and by the time he got ashore they came up with him, this deponent says, they then asked him from whence he came, and what he had in, his answer was the had Plank and Tar, they were from Potomack loaded in the Hungar river and bound to Potomack again. Wheeland then asked this Deponent if he did not belong to the fleet; this Deponent ask'd what fleet? They answered, the English fleet, the deponent answered he did not, he then asked him, who he was for, either the Country or the King, this deponent told him he did

*not choose to inter-meddle with either side, he then asked him how many men he had on board, this deponant told him there was but one person besides himself, he then asked him, this deponant if he were a tory or not, he then told him he could not tell, the said Joseph Wheeland then told him he belonged to the English fleet and he must goe along with him, he then asked him if he was willing to stay with the fleet, he then told him the said Wheeland no, for he had a wife and children, and wanted to get home as soon as possable, the said Wheeland said he would not detain any person that had a family against their will, but if they had no family they should not goe, he then asked him for some victuals for he was very Hungry. He then ordered him to get in the Canoe with the Mulatto fellow Lazarus and goe up to the three Schooners that lay in the Creek, and tell some person to give him some victuals, and while he was giving orders there came two other persons in a Canoe with a Case of Gin & Rum and gave him a dram, he then got out of his Canoe and sent one of the other persons with him, and he the said Wheeland and one of the persons in the other Canoe proceeded on board Cap**Yell. We went some part of the way in the Canoe till they came to an anchor, they then took it in and ordered him to keep along shore, as this deponent was going along, he met with one of the Islanders and had some conversation with him till the said Joseph Wheeland came up with the said Capt Yell, and then took him aboard said canoe and carryd him the said deponent with the said Yell on board the Schooners that lay in the Creeks mouth afs'd in Smyth's Island, where there was likewise a Sloop dismasted as they understood belonged to one White up Nanticoke and when they came aboard they saw about twenty persons sharing of plunder, and as they understood was all County born except one. This deponant with Cap**Yell requested the said Joseph Wheeland to goe on Shore, he told them they might, but that Yell must leave his Cloths on board, they then went on Shore and got some victuals at Richard Evans'. After some time Marmaduke Mister and sundry persons came to the af'sd House and took supper, some time after supper Marmaduke Mister told this deponant and Cap**Yell that they must go abord, for they could not keep guard & ashore too, they then ordered them on board, as they were going along he said (God damn you) do you goe before the guard. John Evans said it would make no difference, he the said Mister said they would not goe before the Guard, when they got aboard they ordered them down in the Cabbin where they remained all night, there were several on the Guard viz. Joseph Wheeland, John Evans, John Price, Robert Howith and one Dial, and several others, that* *he did not know, which said persons as mentioned above is under guard at Hoopers Straights except the said Dial. The next morning Joseph Wheeland ordered three hands to bring up the Vessel, they said when they returned that she was between two bars and they could not get her off. John Evans then persuaded the said Joseph Wheeland to let the men have the Vessel again, as she would not be of any service to them; Wheeland then told the deponent that Capt Yell might have the Vessel if they would get her off, and wanted his said Cloths & money, he then refused him his cloths and Vessel, and said he must have the tar, but if he would waite till he was gone to the fleet he might have the residue of his Cargo and Vessel. The said deponent and Yell went to unloading the s'd Vessel and took out six barrels of tar and put them on board Richard Evan's boat, and told the said Wheeland that he should have the residue as soon as he could come at it. Wheeland told the said Deponent that he had just received orders to come immediately to the fleet, and to burn that Vessel that was understood to be Whites; the said Yell then asked him for his Cloths & money, he then gave him part of his Clothes. And told him some person had stole his money, and that he might have his Vessel and all his load, this Deponant says that he heard the said Joseph Wheeland tell the said Marmaduke Mister that if he would see the afs'd Sloop that belonged to White burnt he might have the iron of s'd vessel, upon which said Vessel was burnt, that the said Joseph Wheeland went off immediately the said Capt. Yell and this deponent hired hands and got off their Vessel and carried her to the Creek afs'd in order to take the remainder of her load and before he had got her loaded two Tenders came in with the Island and the said Deponant Capt Yell went on Shore, and as soon as they got on shore two persons came down the Creek and went on board the said Vessel and carryd her over to the fleet, one of the persons as this deponant was informed was Isaac Summers from Little Annamesick, the other a lad unknown; the afs'd Joseph Wheeland was as the Deponant understood esteemed the Commanding Officer of the said Vessels, and further sayeth not.*

Sworn before Hugh Eccleston

Joseph Mareman lives in St Marys County near Leonard Town on Britons Bay.[84]

Yell's Deposition

July 27 1776

Moses Yell being sworn on the Holy Evangels of Almighty God deposeth and sayeth. That some time about the 15ᵗʰ of this Instant this deponent was going in a vessel on the Potowmack River with Tar and plank but on seeing Dunmore's Fleet this Deponent returned and anchored under Smith's Island. About two or three hours after he had anchored Joseph Wheland with one other man unknown to the Deponent came on board the vessel this deponent was in, & Joseph Wheland asked this Deponent if he saw the Fleet, this Deponent answered he had seen the Fleet & returned in consequence of it. Joseph Wheland then ask'd this Deponent whence he came and where he was bound & who he was for, this Deponent answered he had not a design to kill any person but was a Friend to his Country. Joseph Wheland then asked this Deponent which he thought was right the King or the Shirt Men, this deponent answered he thought the Americans were right Joseph Wheland then told this Deponent he was for the Fleet, and had orders from Ld. Dunmore to take any vessels belonging to the Rebels and destroy such as he thought proper and carry the rest to the Fleet, the sᵈ Wheland then demanded a sight of this Deponents papers which this Deponent gave him, the sᵈ Wheland then took the papers, a pocket book about forty shillings cash and all the cloaths belonging to this Deponant that were in the vessel, except what he had on, and carried this Deponant together with the cloaths and money on board a Tender which he informed this Deponant he had the command of, and likewise the sᵈ Wheland inform'd him he had the command of the other two vessels that were with the one, this Deponent was put on board of. This Deponent sayeth Joseph Wheland told him he had taken a vessel belonging to White in Nanticoke and that he Wheland intended to fit her out with four four pounders, and twelve swivels to guard the Islands and keep the Shirt Men from going on to abuse the Inhabitants, the afᵈ Wheland told him he must take out the mast from his Yell's vessel and put in the vessel he had taken from White which was then driven on ground and had lost her mast, but before he had got her over the Bar, he Yell understood from an old man on board the Tender that Wheland had recᵈ an express from the Fleet ordering him to come up the Potowmac to assist the Fleet in getting water as quick as possible as orders were come to the Fleet to go out, as soon as they cou'd, part to Martinico to fight the French (as they expected a war there) & part to N York or Hallifax. Wheland soon after ordered fire set to White's vessel and one other which he had not got over the Bar, & put this Deponent on shore gave him part of his cloaths and told him he might take his Boat again, this Deponant sayeth that Marmaduke Mister was one of the Persons that kept guard over him on night while he was on board the Tender, the af^d M^r then commanded in the King's name to tell him the truth, this Deponent then told him he was born in this country and had a right to defend his Liberty, Mister then said what those damn'd Rebels call Liberty I call Slavery and so the people will find it, this Deponent further sayeth that Marmaduke Mister set fire to one of the vessels that was burn'd and was to have the Iron for doing it. This Deponent sayeth that John Evans Robert Howith, and one Price were likewise on board the same Tender under the command of the af^d Joseph Wheland (he supposes) as he often heard them call him Captn, this Deponent saith he heard John Evans say he was determined to have several of the principal people on the Islands either dead or alive, or get some of their negroes.

This Deponent saith he has seen Joseph Wheland, John Evans, Robert Howith and Price the four persons above mentioned since they have been under Guard at the Streights and that they are the same persons he saw on board of the Tender mentioned above. This Deponent further saith on his asking Joseph Wheland for his cloths Wheland threatened to put him in Irons in the vessels hole. the Deponent likewise saith that John Evans told him not to be uneasy about his cloaths and money for Wheland would give them to him after he was ready to go from the Island, for the paper money wou'd be of no more use to him than Blank paper.
Sworn before Hugh Eccleston.[85]

Shortly thereafter, Wheland was arrested by Major Daniel Fallin. Wheland and his crew had fallen ill with smallpox, and, drained of energy, they anchored in a creek that flowed into Holland Strait. Being sickly, none of the men could resist the thirty members of Fallin's crew who had come to arrest them for their crimes. Major Fallin had Wheland imprisoned in the Frederick County jail, and then he was transported to the jail in Annapolis to await trial. The Patriot forces recovered a "hogshead and half of rum, thirty bushels of salt, sails, and rigging for a sloop, a large quantity of iron, and a few guns, swords, and cartridge boxes."[86] Wheland admitted that he had traded goods with the British but claimed that the sloop had actually been burned by Lord Dunmore's fleet. Wheland said that he could list witnesses from the Annapolis Bay area that would verify his account. The Council of Maryland determined that it would be too great an effort to track down the listed individuals around that area and thus deprived Wheland of the right to witness testimony.[87] This injustice contributed to the controversy surrounding the legitimacy of the new government and the accountability of due process of law.

The following transcripts are from the Maryland Journal and Correspondence of the Council of Safety concerning this event. They are reproduced in their entirety.

DORCHESTER COUNTY COMMITTEE TO MARYLAND COUNCIL OF SAFETY.

In Committee of Observation, Dorchester County, July 31, 1776

Gent.: We herewith send, under a guard to your Board, Joseph Wheland, Jr, John Evans, and Robert Howith, who were lately taken in Hooper's Streights, in the service of Lord Dunmore, by a party of Majr Fallen's men, and sent by the Major to us, as by his letter, which we have enclosed for your perusal, will appear. The depositions of Joseph Mariman, and Moses Yell, which are mentioned in the enclosed letter, we have since received from Capt Eccleston, the Magistrate who took them, which we have also enclosed. We have not seen Capt Eccleston since he took the depositions, but are informed Mariman and Yell have returned home, on a promise that they will attend your board on notice. We apprehend the Prisoners will not deny their being in the service of Dunmore; but if they should, and any further evidence should be necessary to prove that fact, on your informing us of it we believe such may be easily had.

Wheeland is the man who, the last Convention (as we are told) were informed, served as pilot to Dunmore's vessels up to Nanticoke Point, and he confesses to us he was with the party who took cattle from Hopkins Island.

We are, Gent, your obedt Servants.
Signed pr order of Committee:
Edward Noel, Chairman
To the Honourable the Council of Safety, Annapolis.[88]

Upon his confinement, Joseph Wheland had been stripped of all of his clothing; by the fall, he started to become cold and petitioned the court for garments. He appealed to the court so that he might not suffer through the winter naked and asked that his clothes be returned to him. The following quote is reproduced in its entirety, including grammatical and spelling deviations.

> *The petition of Joseph Whayland Jun' a Languishing Prisoner in the Jail at Annapolis, humbly showeth, that at the time your Petitioner was taken by Maj' Fallin's guard he had all his cloaths taken from him, that he is now naked and has been so ever since his confinement and had not wherewithal to purchase any cloaths; he therefore humbly prays your Honours would be pleased to grant him an order on M' Fallin for the Delivery of his cloaths and your Petitioner as in duty bound shall forever pray.*
> *October 28th 1776.*
> *Joseph Whayland.*[89]

A response was not recorded in the Journal of the Council of Safety, but his petition was granted, and he was provided with adequate attire.[90]

While Joseph Wheland was in captivity, new privateers arose. The most notable picaroon to establish himself during this time was Stephen Mister, the nephew of the aforementioned Marmaduke Mister. In the spring of 1779, Stephen Mister began raiding missions based out of the Annemessex River.[91] It is not known if he had been recruited by his uncle or if he had seen a chance to fill the void while Wheland was incarcerated. The uncle and nephew formed quite a profitable network of privateering. After Stephen Mister confiscated goods, Marmaduke would fence them to make a profit. In actuality, their operation exploited the situation in order to make personal gains rather than support the war effort.

In one week's time, Stephen Mister shut down trade in one part of the bay.

> *Reportedly favoring the waters about the mouth of the Nanticoke, he soon gained a reputation as one of the most active picaroons on the lower Bay. In a single week's raiding, he plundered a plantation on an island near Hooper's Strait, captured more than half a dozen vessels in Tangier Sound, and effectively instituted a total blockade of the Nanticoke.*[92]

The captured vessels were then taken to Smith Island, where Marmaduke would sell them, scrap them or surrender them to the British fleet.

On April 4, 1779, Colonel George Dashiell joined the Maryland schooners *Dolphin* and *Plater* and went in pursuit of Stephen Mister.[93] This was a coordinated effort between the Maryland navy and the militias of Accomack, Worcester, Dorchester and Somerset Counties. They pursued the pirate through the inlets and islands, rivers and marshes. Finally, after twelve days, the party gave up their pursuit when British Royal Navy warships were spotted in the bay. It is suggested that perhaps the privateer sought shelter at his father's house up the Honga River. Stephen Mister's raids continued while Wheland remained in captivity.

Finally, in December 1780, Colonel George Dashiell was contacted by Wheland. After a statement of reconciliation, a £10,000 bond was posted by Samuel Covington and Thomas Holbrook, and Dashiell released the privateer.[94] It was only a short time later that Dashiell received a message that Wheland had plundered and burned the ships of Captain Valentine Peyton, Captain Oakley Haddaway and William Barnes.[95] The privateer had immediately returned to his scathing ways, and Colonels Joseph and George Dashiell continued to pursue Wheland and his privateer fleet.

In February 1781, it is known that Joseph Wheland commanded four barges that raided the banks of the Patuxent River. Within the following five months, he attacked boats on the Wicomico, Potomac and St. Mary's Rivers. Wheland's most villainous act was reported by John Anderson, a British deserter from the *Resolution*, who testified that the captain and his mates conducted a heinous attack against the widow Elsey Evans.[96]

Wheland continued to plunder the Eastern Shore and apprehended vessels sailing on the Chesapeake. At this point, he raided both Patriot and Loyalist vessels. Colonel Dashiell realized the folly of releasing the criminal and contacted Maryland governor Thomas Sim Lee on March 4, 1781:

> *Joseph Whalland that old offender is down in Somerset plundering Again and we have reason to believe that the Gaoler in Baltimore is alone to blame as Wheland's Father informed one of our Neighbours that he let him go at large sum time before he Came away if this practice is followed no one will venture to take any of them up and send them forward as they will be there to suffer for it. If I had Directions to go into Somerset, I think I could apprehend him, as he had lately robbed a certain Thomas Reuker who I think would assist me to Trap him…whenever your Excellency & Council propose to Remove the people and stock of the Islands I should be Glad to assist with all my heart as I consider them at this time the most Dangerous Enemy we have to watch the Motions off- and am Certain if*

they Can do us no other Damage they will rob & Plunder all they Can before they are removed.[97]

When forces started to close in on Wheland's team of picaroons, he and his first mate, Michael Timmons, fled to North Carolina.[98] They were eventually captured by North Carolinian authorities in 1781, and Maryland petitioned for extradition to bring them back to the state for trial. While the extradition party was traveling from Maryland, the two managed to escape from the authorities.

One of Wheland's most embarrassing circumstances occurred in the fall of 1781. Captain John Greenwood was sailing a forty-ton trading schooner from Baltimore to the Piankatank River and delivered a load of cargo. When they exited the river, they found the wind and tide unfavorable, so they anchored for the night.[99] On board were seven rum traders who were supplying Washington's army and were happy to oblige the men with some libations for the night. Two British galleys anchored nearby went unnoticed by Greenwood's crew. Greenwood, feeling drowsy, told another sailor to take the helm while he went below deck and wrapped himself in his "greatcoat" in order to rest upon the supply of oats in the hold.[100] While he slept, the two British galleys—a thirty-man vessel captained by a mulatto named George and a sixty-man galley captained by none other than Joseph Wheland—approached the unsuspecting schooner and boarded it.[101] A tussle soon ensued between the boarding party and the drunken revelers. Greenwood was awakened by the loud commotion on deck and shouted to his partying comrades to quiet down. At that moment, a man jumped down into the hold and forced the captain up onto the deck at sword point.

Upon entering into the light, Captain Greenwood recognized the man as someone named "Montgomery."[102] It was at this point that Captain Greenwood met Captain Joseph Wheland and described him as thus:

He was a tall, slim, gallows looking fellow, in his shirt sleeves, with a gold-laced jacket on that he had robbed from some old trooper on the eastern shore. "Sir," said he, "I will let you know that I have as good a commission as any seventy-four in his Brittanic Majesty's service!" I told him that I had…thought at first it was one of our own gallies from Annapolis, who would at times board and plunder even our own vessels.[103]

Both men stood eye-to-eye and looked each other up and down. In an act of leniency, Wheland allowed Greenwood to keep his clothing, including the greatcoat he had been using as bedding. He ordered Captain

George to use the smaller galley to tow in the schooner with a grappling hook in order to confiscate and unload her cargo. Greenwood and his first mate remained on board the schooner along with Captain George and Montgomery as well as a few other armed picaroons. In the meantime, Wheland sailed up the Piankatank River to seize the goods that Captain Greenwood had just delivered.

On board the schooner, only Captain Greenwood and his mate remained along with their captors: Captain George, Montgomery, a helmsman and another man by the foremast. Captain Greenwood devised a plan to retake the schooner from the four armed guards. He convinced Captain George that there was a stash of money that had been hidden inside of the cabin. The gullible man immediately went into the cabin to find the loot. Greenwood colorfully explained what happened next.

> *As I stood by the cabin door I called Montgomery to me, and as he came near, seized him by the collar, tripped him up with my feet, and pitched him into the cabin, at the same time my partner caught up the cutlass, which the man at the helm had carelessly left on the stern-sheets, and running forward struck down the man there. The helmsman now cried out, "Heim! Heim!" which was all he had time to say, for W____b was aft again in an instant with his cutlass raised, just going to strike him in the head: he had however at the first alarm hauled out the tiller and made a stroke at me, it missed and dropped out of his hand, when seeing no chance of safety, the fellow… jumped over the stern of the vessel into the water. As the man could not swim I suppose he drowned…*
>
> *At this time the galley in tow was so near that I could have jumped on board her, and the fire of the muskets almost burned my hair, but they were…bad marksmen…I had entirely forgotten the grapnel in our stern-sheets…I took it up and threw it over exclaiming "There, my boys, you have got your galley all to yourselves!" at the same time they were firing right at me, saying: "Fire at that fellow with a great coat on!"*[104, 105]

The schooner did manage to escape, and Captain Greenwood helped treat any wounds that Captain George and Montgomery had received. Arrangements were agreed upon in which prisoners were exchanged.

Wheland's last major known raid was at the town of Benedict up the Patuxent River on February 17, 1783. He had constructed a barracks along Kedges Straits and raised a considerable force.[106] His shipmate raided and burned the house of Benjamin Mackall at Hallowing Point on the opposite side of the river. Meanwhile, Wheland raided the home and warehouse of Phillip Ferguson, who questioned him, "Did you not raid me prior?" To mock the man and force him to remember, Wheland wrote upon his wall in bright red letters: "Joseph Wayland Commander of the Sloop *Rover*."[107] After eluding militia forces, this would be one of Wheland's last raids during the Revolution.

Wheland's fate is not fully recorded, but it is steeped in local legends of the islanders. There is a story that between the end of the Revolution and the War of 1812, many of the Loyalists in the area were imprisoned, fined or forced to take oaths of allegiance, and perhaps some of the more severe offenders received worse punishments. Rumor has it that "Tory Jo Whalen" managed to escape and sought concealment amongst the swamps and morasses of Tangier Island. He supposedly lived a recluse's life, surviving on just the natural vegetation and aquatic life in the region of the backwaters. In this confined and isolated environment, he was eventually driven mad and had fits of severe torment in which he would scream all night long. His cries were so agonizing that the residents of the island were often awakened in the middle of the night due to the loud shrieks and rantings of the lunatic. One day, the terrifying howling ceased, and a search team cautiously ventured toward the remote regions of the Tangier Island marshes.

> *When his body was found, he was so emaciated that he "resembled neither man nor any of God's creatures…Some islanders refused to believe he was dead for many years; when the wind blew at midnight, they, in their imagination could still hear screams off in a distance and arose from their beds to make sure that doors and shutters were securely latched."*[108]

The effects of Loyalist privateers upon the farmers and sailors of the Eastern Shore were devastating to the economy and livelihood of the residents. While the British were encouraging this pillaging, Patriot forces were also expecting provisions to support the Continental army and the militias. The goods of the residents of this area were being confiscated, and in many cases, those affected were provided with currency that amounted to little more than promissory notes. Picaroons such as Joseph Wheland, Richard Evans, Marmaduke Mister and Stephen Mister plundered plantations up and down the bay and disrupted much of the maritime trade during this time. It appears understandable why some of the locals did not care for either side of the war effort. What is even more disturbing is that these picaroons were so devious and violent they continued to haunt the imaginations of local residents from beyond the grave.

PART FOUR

ZEDEKIAH WHALEY
AND JOHN CROPPER

B etween 1778 and 1779, the Maryland state government found that it had insufficient funds to support the cost of its navy despite its miniscule size. The colonial government turned its focus toward supporting the militias' efforts to protect farmland and securing the resources needed to fund the war effort. The state sold the *Defence*, the *Baltimore* and the *Johnson*, as well as two other vessels that were being built that had not yet been commissioned.[109] As one might imagine, the Loyalist privateers went about plundering coastal villages and islands unchecked. The commanders of the Dorchester, Worcester and Somerset Militias were unable to keep up with the hit-and-run tactics of these marauders and implored the Annapolis government for maritime military support:[110]

> *Whereas the Enemy have fitted out a Number of small Vessels to ravage &*
> *plunder our Farms & Plantations which lie on the Water & have lately*
> *plundered many of our Countrymen and burnt & destroyed their Houses*
> *threatening the like Destruction wherever they shall be able to effect it with*
> *Security — And whereas from the present exhausted State of the public*
> *Treasury Government cannot immediately give that Protection…a Water*
> *Defence is the best & most effective Way of preventing those Surprizes*
> *Depredations & Ravages.*[111]

Regardless of their shrinking treasury, the Maryland Council of Safety saw that this battle would be futile without dominion of the Chesapeake

Bay and passed the Bay Defence Act of October 1780, which authorized Governor Thomas Sim Lee to spend money in order to raise a proper navy.[112] The governor immediately set about to increase the naval forces and built a new galley and a number of low-draft barges that could help patrol the shoal waters and inlets of the bay. By this time, the schooner *Venus*, a boat named *Dolphin* and the barges *Revenge*, *Terrible*, *Intrepid*, *Reformation* and the *Fearnaught* were commissioned by the Maryland government.[113] Some of these vessels were most likely ships from the local area that were already constructed or captured from the British but were now commissioned into the Maryland navy. Additionally, some of the local sailors petitioned the governor and the state council to construct ships for the new fleet. For instance, in Talbot and Queen Anne's County, the residents built the barge *Experiment*, and in Dorchester County, residents constructed the barge *Defence* at their own expense.[114] While they had a willingness to construct a force for the colonial navy, this did not mean that all of the ships' owners were supportive of the new government. Like their Loyalist counterparts, they, too, were interested in the privateering business with the expectation of retaining private ownership of the vessel after the conclusion of the war. The new Maryland naval force soon faced its bloodiest engagement in what many consider one of the fiercest battles fought on the Chesapeake Bay and the last naval engagement of the Revolutionary War.

Lord Charles Cornwallis, the 2nd Earl of Cornwallis, officially surrendered at the Battle of Yorktown, Virginia, on October 19, 1781. At the siege of Yorktown, nearly five hundred British soldiers were killed, and about seven thousand surrendered to American and French forces. Lord Cornwallis capitulated and asked for the traditional rights of honor to march his troops from the battlefield. Washington rejected the proposition, claiming that the British had refused the same honor for the American forces during past defeats. The conditions of the surrender granted to the British were that they could march in retreat but could not bear flags or arms and could not play tribute music for the victors. On the day of surrender, Cornwallis refused to attend or, as other accounts attest, claimed he was ill. His deputy came forward to the American and French forces and symbolically offered his sword in surrender to the French marshal Jean-Baptiste Donatien de Vimeur, Comte de Rochambeau, who refused to accept the sword. He indicated to approach American general George Washington, who also refused to accept the British surrender. The second-in-command to Cornwallis finally surrendered his sword to the second-in-command to Washington—this being a military sign of "courteous disrespect" between the commanders of the opposing sides.

The British retreated without any flags and laid down their muskets before the French and American forces. The following painting is found in the rotunda of the U.S. Capitol and depicts the French on the left displaying a white flag representing the Bourbon dynasty, while in the middle, American general Benjamin Lincoln extends his hand to accept the sword from British general Charles O'Hara. Washington remained mounted in the rear and refused to accept the surrender since Cornwallis himself was not present.

While most colonists thought the Revolutionary War was over, this was not necessarily the case in the Chesapeake Bay and on the Eastern Shore of Virginia and Maryland. Since no official treaty had been drawn and signed, battles continued to be fought in this area for over a year after the surrender at Yorktown. The inhabitants of the area had been considerably lawless during the conflict, and this surrender did not change their activities. The privateering on the bay and the raiding of farms still continued after the ceremonial cessation of war.

The Battle of the Barges was a famous naval engagement conducted on the Chesapeake Bay in November 1782 and involved commissioned barges and other privateering vessels. This battle marked not only one of the last battles of the war but one of the bloodiest naval conflicts during the Revolution. There were several notable officers who were influential during this confrontation, but the two most prominent men were Commodore Zedekiah Whaley, of the Maryland State Navy, and Lieutenant Colonel John Cropper from Accomack County, Virginia. These two men actually fought together on the *Protector* during the Battle of the Barges. It may have been the tenacity of these two American commanders that escalated this battle to become one of the most gruesome confrontations on the Chesapeake Bay. Before examining the details of the battle, the backgrounds of these two officers should be examined.

On March 21, 1781, William Winder and others from Somerset County, Maryland, proposed to the Maryland Council to have Captain Whaley construct a fifty-foot barge to carry sixty men and a twenty-four pound gun in order to patrol the bay's waters.[115] The council responded to their request with an astonishing admission that the state was destitute and could not finance any future shipbuilding efforts. The local citizens rallied Captain Whaley to commence with the construction of the new vessel despite the lack of funds. Whaley "is said to have been a very brave man, but unnecessarily rash and ungovernable."[116] The barge, the *Protector*, was constructed by Whaley in Worcester County at Snow Hill. It seems that shipbuilders petitioned local residents for the needed material, and within

Surrender of Lord Cornwallis by John Trumbull, 1820. This painting is on display in the rotunda of the U.S. Capitol in Washington, D.C. *Courtesy of the Architect of the Capitol.*

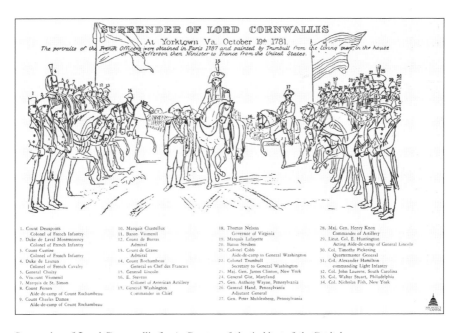

Surrender of Lord Cornwallis (key). *Courtesy of the Architect of the Capitol.*

a short matter of time, obtained all of the provisions that were required for the vessel's construction. By June 16, 1781, the *Protector* was ready to sail, and the Maryland Council granted a commission to Commodore Whaley and his first lieutenant, Joseph Handy, to command the Maryland fleet.[117] Within the first two months, a progress report to Governor Thomas Sim Lee indicated that Commodore Whaley had driven many of the Loyalist privateers into hiding and had already captured two vessels.[118] On July 31, 1782, the Maryland Council confirmed that Commodore Whaley was in charge of the Chesapeake Bay's barge fleet and determined the ranking of the fleet's captains to be in the order of Robert Dashiell, Solomon Frazier and Levin Spedden, with Levin Handy commanding the marines on the *Protector*.[119]

The co-commander during the Battle of the Barges was Colonel John Cropper. Cropper's previous military background alone warrants an in-depth investigation of his incredible advances in rank and ferocity. Cropper was born on December 23, 1755, at Joynes Neck in Accomack County, Virginia.[120] He began his military career in 1775, and in 1776, he received his first commission as a captain in a company of the 9th Virginia Regiment. Within one year, he was promoted to a major of the 5th Virginia Regiment.[121] Before he received a chance to acclimate to his new position, in September 1777, he fought under the command of George Washington at Brandywine Creek in Chester County, Pennsylvania. Specifically, Major Cropper was under the command of Brigadier General William Woodford of the Virginia Brigade.

The Battle of Brandywine was a turning point in the military career of John Cropper. Chaplain Jeremias Trout rallied the troops the night before the battle, during which he stated:

> *We have met this evening perhaps for the last time…alike we have endured the cold and hunger…the sunlight that, tomorrow morn, will glimmer on scenes of blood…. in time of terror and gloom, have gathered together, God grant it may not be the last time…the heights of the Brandywine arise gloomily beyond yonder stream--all nature pauses in solemn silence, on the eve of tomorrow. Tomorrow morning we will go forth to battle…Many of us may fall.*[122]

The fighting commenced early on the misty day of September 11, 1777, and lasted for a grueling eleven hours of continuous combat. It was the longest-lasting single-day engagement of the war. The battle itself was quite

Portrait of General Cropper by Charles Willson Peale, 1793. *Courtesy of the Division of Political History, National Museum of American History, Smithsonian Institution, Washington, D.C.*

a disaster for the Americans, and the survivors of Cropper's regiment, wet and wounded, had to take shelter in the bushes on the battlefield for the night. During this conflict, Cropper incurred a non-life-threatening bayonet wound to the leg. Amidst the battle, the flag bearer carrying the regiment's colors had been struck by a musket ball, and Chaplain Trout was killed, thereby fulfilling his own prophecy.

At first light, Major Cropper grabbed a musket ramrod, tied a red cloth to it and rushed to the front of his men, using the ramrod as his regiment's flag. As the standard-bearer, he led his men safely in retreat. He heroically guided his remaining troops back to General Washington. When Generals Washington and Woodford saw Cropper limping across Chester Brandywine Bridge carrying a makeshift flag, they were stunned—they had not known that his men had sought concealment for the night and assumed that all had perished in the battle. General Woodford rode up to Cropper, jumped off of his horse, embraced his comrade and exclaimed, "[H]e whom we thought was lost, is found!"[123]

Woodford was one of the unfortunate souls to have perished aboard a British prison ship. It has been estimated that more colonial soldiers died while in captivity than died on the battlefield. One of the deadliest British prison ships at that time was the HMS *Jersey*, based in New York, which could hold over one thousand prisoners. General Woodford was captured at the Seize of Charleston in the spring of 1780 and confined to a British prison hulk off of the coast of New York. Almost eight thousand American captives perished aboard New York and New Jersey prison hulks, including William Woodford, who died on November 13, 1780.

After spending the winter of 1777–78 at Valley Forge, on June 28, 1778, John Cropper fought alongside General George Washington at the Battle of Monmouth. He served as the interim commander of the 11th Virginia regiment.[124] While he was in this relief position, he officiated a court martial of a Virginia officer accused of gambling in camp. Washington addressed the soldiers and berated them, stating that a military base was no place to have any gaming or gambling and they should conduct themselves as gentlemen. As he left, Washington reminded them that there were still a few Continental lottery tickets available for purchase at the camp's headquarters.[125] While this story is amusing, the actual battle was quite harsh. According to accounts, due to the extreme heat and the heaviness of uniforms and gear, many soldiers died from heat exhaustion and dehydration. Soldiers were unable to get fresh water or any relief from the heat. The conditions were so deplorable that, according to one account from a reputable officer, Washington confronted General Charles Lee and swore to Lee's face "like an angel."[126]

Shortly after this, Cropper received word from home that British raiders and privateers were ransacking and burning homes up and down the Eastern Shore. Cropper sought permission to leave in order to return to Accomack County, Virginia, to check on the situation and the safety of his

Bowman's Folly, Accomack County. After the raid on the house, it was rebuilt in about 1815 and is listed in the National Register of Historic Places. *Courtesy of the Library of Congress, Prints and Photographs Division, Jack Boucher, HABS, VA, 1-AC. V, 1-2.*

family. In September 1778, he was granted leave to investigate the damage of the raiding parties and the welfare of his family.[127]

Colonel Cropper arrived at his estate, Bowman's Folly, in Accomack County, Virginia, to find his wife, Margaret "Peggy" Pettit, and their eighteen-month-old daughter, Sarah Corbin, safe for the moment.[128] This was the first time that he had held his daughter, who had been named after his uncle, Colonel George Corbin, and was born after he left for military service.[129] He heard of the pillaging and damage that the privateers had caused to his neighbors. This ignited Cropper's obsession with the elimination of the privateering movement. The colonel did not know that the repercussions of his decision would strike so close to home. The return to his estate coincided with the raid of his residence by Loyalist pirates.

According to Cropper's journal entry dated February 12, 1779, the British privateering vessel the *Thistle* tender, a Bermudian sloop commanded by Captain Thomas Byron Williams and piloted by a man named Dunton, stealthily rowed up Folly Creek at Joynes Neck in the middle of the night and headed toward the colonel's house.[130, 131] While all the members of the family were sound asleep in their beds, the raiders burst through the door and quickly rushed into the house. Colonel Cropper defended his home against these invaders while his wife and daughter rushed away into the darkness of the night. It was not known if there would be other assailants waiting outside to take them away, and the fate of the colonel was in the hands of the ruffians. He was secured in a room and forced to remain captive with his only way out guarded by two armed men.

While John Cropper was confined, he did not know the whereabouts of his wife and child—or his own fate, for that matter. All he could do was listen to the raiders plunder his house and break his furniture and windows. Unbeknownst to him, the men started to lay a line of gunpowder from the house back to their privateer vessel anchored on the bank of Folly Creek. It was only a matter of time before the picaroons would grab every last piece of loot from the house and then ignite it with Colonel John Cropper trapped inside.

As Cropper waited in confinement, he started to notice sounds of merriment amongst the men. The raiders had discovered the most desirable item in the house—the wine cellar. The privateers started to imbibe the Croppers' collection of wine and spirits. During this moment of jubilant thievery of libations, Colonel Cropper decided to make his escape. While his captors were distracted by the events and the liquor, Cropper quietly raised the latch of the door and jumped over the heads of his guards, who were on the floor. John Cropper escaped from his house dressed only in his nightgown and ran two miles to his closest neighbor's house. He convinced his neighbor to give him "Tower" muskets (also known as "Brown Bess" muskets hallmarked at the Tower of London), and the two then headed back to Bowman's Folly. However, upon approaching the Cropper residence, the neighbor heard the number of men inside and fled in fear. The colonel was left alone with two single-shot muskets; this was certainly no match for the number of men inside of the house.

The colonel was in a dire situation; his home was being vandalized, and the whereabouts of his wife and daughter were unknown. He was desperate to find his family and did not care that his personal belongings were being stolen and destroyed. The raiders had bound and taken approximately thirty of Cropper's slaves and loaded them aboard the *Thistle*, so Cropper was alone.[132] He did not have any additional men nor enough firepower to overtake the pillagers. As an army officer, he probably would have considered ordering his soldiers to wait for reinforcements, but as a husband and father, there was no doubt in his mind about his course of action. He chose to fight the pirates singlehandedly.

John Cropper wanted to convince the pirates that he had sought reinforcements, so he stormed up to his house and yelled at the top of his lungs. He then fired the only two shots he had and screamed, "Come on boys, we have got them now!"[133] Deceived by this ruse, the sailors fled from the fictional defenders and returned to the *Thistle* tender down at the creek. Cropper found that the raiders never had a chance to ignite the line of gunpowder. Had his captors not discovered the stash of alcohol in the cellar, the colonel most certainly would have perished.

Cropper's wife and young daughter were nowhere to be found, and the traumatized man found only the destruction of busted windowpanes and stolen property. It turned out his family's fate was far worse than Cropper's—they had spent the whole night in the outhouse. While no harm came to them, the night of terror and hiding in stench must have been nearly unbearable. Considering Bowman's Folly was basically destroyed, the colonel moved his family to another property he owned, the Latin House, which was located farther inland near the courthouse.

The perpetrators of this raid were able to escape unharmed, but this crime inflamed in the colonel a rage against the privateers that ultimately led to their demise. On Wednesday, February 24, 1779, Cropper planned an expedition to find Captain Thomas Byron Williams at Cedar Island, but he was not able to confront the pirate on that day. On Saturday, February 27, he received a knock on his door at ten at night; Colonel George Corbin, Cropper's uncle, had the *Thistle* tender pinned down at Parramore's Beach.[134] Immediately, Cropper raised a force to encounter the vessel. On February 28, Colonel Cropper got retribution for the invasion of his home when he fired upon the *Thistle*. Unwisely, the ship sailed out to sea after being badly damaged. Even with men pumping the water that was flooding into the hull, the ship sank with all souls on board while the residents of Accomack County witnessed the event from the shore. This one victory might have sufficed to deliver some relief after the personal attack against his family and home, but it did not extinguish Cropper's hatred for the privateering fleet.

Perhaps due to his bravery at Brandywine or the sinking of the *Thistle*, on March 20, 1779, Cropper was informed he would be elevated to the rank of lieutenant colonel of the 7th Regiment of the Virginian Militia in Accomack County.[135] Cropper and his wife returned to live at Bowman's Folly on April 24, and a galley, the *Diligence*, was positioned at the mouth of

Folly Creek in Metompkin Bay to prevent any further invasions. The couple became friends with the captain of that galley, Captain Watson, and were frequent dinner guests aboard his galley. Cropper was to officially take his position on October 27, after his furlough, but the previous attack on his family gave him reservations. Even with the added security measure of a galley, on August 16, 1779, Cropper presented his official resignation to John Jay, the president of Congress.

> *I had the honor to be appointed a Captain in the Virginia line of the Continental Army, and have served until I have attained the rank of Lieutenant-Colonel; but my affairs at home together with the present establishment of the army absolutely demand that I should quit that service, in which I have spent the most happy and honorable part of my life; therefore, I humbly and earnestly request permission to resign.*[136]

In a rare circumstance, Congress refused his resignation and granted him an indefinite leave of absence. In August 1781, Governor Thomas Nelson Jr. appointed him the county lieutenant of Accomack County, and he was allowed to retain his commission throughout the entire war while serving only in his home county.[137]

PART FIVE

BATTLE OF THE BARGES

I n the spring of 1782, Colonel Joseph Dashiell of Worcester County, Colonel George Dashiell of Somerset County, Colonel Henry Hooper of Dorchester County and Colonel Richard Barnes of St. Mary's County all petitioned the Maryland Council for funds to combat the Loyalist privateers, which resulted in the passage of the Act for the Protection of the Bay Trade on May 22.[138] By September, Commodore Zedekiah Whaley had returned to Baltimore with four vessels that he had recaptured from Loyalist privateers. His ambition was well noticed by the state government, and on September 24, 1782, the Maryland Council ordered Commodore Whaley to eradicate the British privateers in the Chesapeake Bay.[139] Whaley waited in Baltimore to rendezvous with the French fleet and the American barge, *Fearnaught*. The council, unaware of the strategic logistics of the operation, ordered Whaley to set sail on September 26, before his vessel had time to properly store cargo, which would turn out to be a critical mistake.[140] Finally, on September 28, the barge *Fearnaught* arrived, and the council ordered Whaley to sail out of port for a third time. Reluctantly, without the French support, Whaley set sail from Baltimore.

Commodore Whaley had command of four sail and oar barges and an armed schooner. The schooner, *Flying Fish*, was commanded by Captain Daniel Bryan, who was charged with traveling quickly to bring supplies and communiques to and from the barges. The barges were heavily armed, and while they could not travel fast, their shallow draft made them ideal for traveling in the marshy inlets of the islands and tributaries. The four barges included the *Fearnaught*, commanded by Captain Levin Spedden; the *Defence*, commanded by Captain Solomon Frazier; the *Terrible*, commanded by Captain Robert Dashiell; and the flagship, the *Protector*, which was commanded by Commodore Whaley himself.[141] By late October 1782, the council gave no indication that they had heard from the French regarding the possibility of any reinforcements.

In early November, Commodore Whaley's flotilla took up residence in Onancock Creek in order to monitor the traffic of Loyalist privateers. Whaley learned on November 12 that at least five British barges were entering the bay from the sea. The commodore, a very strategic sailor, calculated their course and sought to intercept them. Whaley's fleet made a significant capture off of Gwynn's Island on November 15. The Loyalist barge, *Jolly Tar*, commanded by Captain Daniel I. Brooks, was pursued and eventually captured by Captain Frazier of the *Defence*.[142] The rest of the flotilla pursued a second vessel for over fifty miles until it reached the mouth of the Chesapeake and continued to sail up the Atlantic coast. They followed the vessel into the open ocean; however, as dusk approached, the ships returned to the safety of the bay. The capture of the *Jolly Tar* was a short-lived victory, but it would turn out to be a crucial one following the Battle of the Barges.

On November 28, 1782, Commodore Whaley encountered Captain John Kidd and Joseph Wheland in the Tangier Sound off of Onancock; he found himself outnumbered by six British barges.[143] The commander, a normally brash man, was forced to take refuge in Onancock Creek.[144] He managed to notify Colonel John Cropper, of Accomack County, Virginia, about the situation, and Cropper was able to assemble twenty-five additional men to sail captured British vessels the *Victory* and a much smaller barge called *Langodoc*.

The next day, Commodore Whaley sent Captain Frazier of the *Defence* to sail under British colors to inquire of the local colonists as to the movement of any naval vessels that had been there the day before.[145] Frazier hurried back to inform Commodore Whaley, who was still stationed between the mouth of the Onancock River and Watt's Island.[146] The local Loyalists, unsuspecting of the deception, indicated the British had sailed in the direction of Kedges Straits. The British ships commanded by Commodore John Kidd were seen near Tangier Island, and a pursuit ensued.[147, 148] Now with additional men, the colonial forces headed back into the bay. Unfortunately, to the dismay of the Maryland navy, the *Victory* ran aground at the mouth of the Onancock River, some twenty miles away, and Commodore Whaley ordered her to

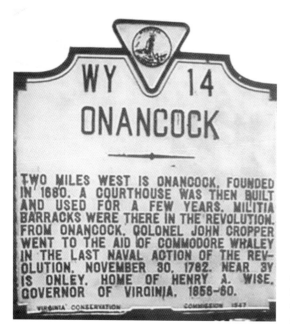

Onancock, cropped from the original image. *Courtesy of the Virginia Department of Historic Resources.*

return back to port. The commodore's forces were now again down a vessel, but the remaining vessels were under solid command. The colonel and some other officers joined Whaley on his flagship, the *Protector*. Cropper assumed the role as second-in-command on the *Protector*, while Lieutenant Samuel Handy and Continental army captain Levin Handy, the commander of the marines on the *Protector*, assumed command of the *Langodoc*.[149]

With the *Protector* being far in advance of the rest of the fleet, Colonel Cropper implored the commodore to wait to make an advance until the slower sailing barges were able to rendezvous with them.[150] Whaley ignored this suggestion and proceeded with an attack on Captain Kidd's vessels. On November 30, 1782, the Patriot forces finally caught up to Kidd's forces at Cager's Strait (now called Kedges Straits) between the north side of Smith Island and South Marsh Island.[151] Captain Kidd saw that the *Protector* was vulnerable and ordered his fleet to turn about and engage the ship. By the time the British had closed ranks, the *Fearnaught* and the *Defence* had managed to draw abreast to the flagship. Strangely, Captain Robert Dashiell positioned the *Terrible* well to the rear of the engagement, perhaps to serve as a line of defense for the supply schooner, the *Flying Fish*.[152] At about 9:30 a.m., when the two opposing sides had approached to within two to three hundred yards of each other, the British opened fire with a barrage of cannon and musket fire primarily focused on the *Protector*.[153] The Americans forced four of the British ships to retreat, but it was a brief reprieve.[154]

During the confusion of this confrontation, gunpowder spilled onto the deck of the *Protector*, and as Whaley screamed to wet the powder, it ignited the stern powder magazine, which in turn caused the midship powder magazine to explode in a massive ball of fire with a deafening roar, immediately killing four men and forcing others to jump overboard engulfed in flames.[155] Sailors were left in the water holding on to the side rigging of the ship to save their lives.[156] Even with the *Protector* critically damaged, Cropper still engaged the enemy forces. The commodore's stubbornness would not let him recognize the futile situation, and his decision would soon put the fate of his ship and crew—and even his own life—in jeopardy. Perhaps if the council had permitted sufficient time to properly stow the munitions, this accident might have been avoided. A definitive reason was never determined as to how the powder that caused this powerful explosion was spilled.

Four of the British barges sought to intercept and deflect any of the colonial barges coming to the aid of the *Protector* during this devastating calamity.[157] Fearing that they would be overpowered, the three other colonial barges fled, leaving only the *Protector*. The sixty-five person crew, including Commodore Whaley, Colonel Cropper, Major Smith Snead, Captain Thomas Parker and Captain William Snead, were left to fend for themselves. Most of the colonial fleet was pursued up the bay, while the supply schooner, *Flying Fish*, and its defense barge, *Langodoc*, sought refuge by sailing up the Annemessex River.[158] Captain Levin Handy, aboard the *Langodoc*, received seven separate wounds.

Whaley, Cropper and all the other crewmen of the *Protector* soon found themselves surrounded by the British barges. Commodore Whaley refused to surrender to Commodore John Kidd and ordered his crew to not lower their colors, which resulted in the ensuing battle.[159] During this confrontation, Commodore Whaley was fatally wounded when a musket ball tore through his chest. First Lieutenant (or captain, in some accounts) Joseph Handy had his arm completely blown off but continued to fight until he was ultimately killed.[160] All of their supporting vessels had retreated, leaving the *Protector* to defend itself. Ironically, this placed Colonel Cropper, who was not a trained naval commander, in command of the flagship.[161] Without any escape, the only solution was to either surrender or fight to the death. With the recent attack on his family still fresh in his mind, Cropper decided to follow Whaley's orders and continued to put up a resistance and refused to lower his colors. He held his place in the hope that the other three barges would return with reinforcements.

The Loyalists from the *Kidnapper* boarded the *Protector*, and with the ship being completely engulfed in flames, Colonel Cropper proceeded to fight the raiders in hand-to-hand combat. Amongst the blazing fire, he engaged the enemy, which resulted in Cropper being horrendously wounded with a sabre cut across his scalp.[162] Cropper was solely fighting two white men and one African American man by defending himself with a musket and bayonet. He would have been killed had it not been for one of his father's slaves. The African American he was fighting had been in the service of Cropper's family, but he was now fighting with Captain Kidd and his forces.[163] "In the middle of this individual contest, the negro discovering his young master to be the person with whom he and the two whitemen were engaged, cried out, 'Save him; he is my young master!'"[164] The man drew his sword against the invading soldiers and declared, "My God, Massa John; and I will die before they shall lay hands on him."[165] An Irishman who had previously been Cropper's prisoner also came to his defense and declared, "I am with you," due to the compassion he had received from the colonel while he was in captivity.[166] In thanks for saving his life, Cropper later declared the escaped slave a free man and helped establish him in Baltimore.

Cropper and Captain Handy were badly wounded, but the British privateer force saw fit to save their lives and brought them aboard one of the Loyalist barges. Captain Thomas Parker and Major Smith Snead also survived and were taken prisoner by Captain Kidd. Kidd himself was wounded during the battle and had twenty-two dead or wounded men aboard his vessel. All of the survivors from the *Protector* were transferred to the *Kidnapper* and transported to Onancock. When Commodore Whaley had called upon the militia for reinforcements, Major Snead did not have time to change into his military uniform and was forced to set sail wearing civilian clothes. On the other hand, his subordinate, Captain Parker, was wearing his captain's uniform. In a bit of irony, Captain Kidd invited Captain Parker to dine with him, and as they passed Snead, Kidd shoved him out of the way and said "in the roughest manner, 'Get out of the way, you d----d rebel, and let the *Captain* [emphasis added] pass.'"[167] Parker did not want to give away the identity of Snead, so he and the major maintained this pretense for the entire time they were in captivity.

Colonel Cropper was placed at the stern of one of the Loyalist ships. He was in such a weak condition that he barely noticed the man next to him struggle to get up and look at him. The man himself was so wounded that it took several attempts to gain enough strength to get enough leverage to see Cropper. Once he recognized Colonel Cropper, he grabbed the closest available weapon, a gun rammer, in order to kill him:

> *One of his assailants, while in the act of dealing a blow with a heavy gun-rammer, had his lower jaw entirely carried away by a shot; but in the agony of death, as if by a violent spasmodic effort, he brought down the whole force of his frantic strength upon Cropper's already wounded head. This sent the latter to the bottom of the barge, apparently dead.*[168]

According to reports, this blow sent the colonel into unconsciousness, possibly facing death.

A letter dated December 6, 1782, and addressed to Colonel William Davies better explains the confrontation in Cropper's own recollection of the events:

> *Dear Sir*
>
> *On the 28th ultimo, I received a letter from Commodore Whaley, requesting a number of militia to full man his fleet, in consequence of his intention to attack the enemy's barges then off Onancock. In compliance with which request, on the 29th I went on board his fleet myself, with twenty-five volunteers of the Accomac militia. On the 30th, at the head of Cagey's Straits (or Kedges) we fell in with and engaged the enemy. When we approached them, within about three hundred yards, and the fire began to be serious our barges all ran away except the Commodore's, the "Protector," in which was Major Smith Snead, Captain Thomas Parker, Captain William Snead, myself and five other volunteers. This dastardly conduct of our comrades brought on our barge the whole fire of the enemy, which was severe, and it was as severely answered by the Protector, until the enemy's six barges were within fifty yards, when most unfortunately the cartridges of our short eighteen-pounders caught fire amid-ships; the explosion of which burned three or four people to death, and caused five or six more, all a-fire to leap overboard, and the alarm of the barges' blowing up made several others swim for their lives. The enemy almost determined to retreat from our fire, as they told us afterwards, took new spirits at this disaster and pushed up with redoubled fury. On the other hand, our people opposed them with the most daring resolution. There was one continued shower of musket balls, boarding pikes, cutlass, cold shot and iron stansails, for*

eight or ten minutes till greatly overpowered by numbers, and having all the officers on the barge killed and wounded, we struck to them, after having wounded their Commodore, killed one Captain, wounded another, killed and wounded several of their inferior officers, and killed and wounded fifteen of the Kidnapper's crew, the barge which first boarded us. Commodore Whaley was shot down a little before the enemy boarded, acting the part of a cool, intrepid, gallant officer; Captain Joseph Handy fell nigh the same time, nobly fighting with one arm after the loss of the other- Captain Levin Handy was badly wounded. There went to action in the Protector sixty-five men; twenty-five of them were killed and drowned, twenty-nine were wounded, some of whom are since dead and eleven only escaped being wounded, most of whom leaped into the water to save themselves from the explosion. At the foot you have a particular account of the loss sustained by the volunteers on board the Protector. After the surrender I entered into an agreement with Commodore Kidd to take ashore such of his wounded as chose to go and to have them nursed and attended, at the public expense, upon condition that he would parole all our prisoners, as well the unhurt as wounded; which agreement I hope will meet the approbation of his Excellency in Council and the Assembly. Being very much disordered .with my wounds, I am scarcely able to write, therefor I beg leave to subscribe myself, Your most respectful servant, John Cropper, Jnr....

Myself was wounded by a cutlass on the head, slightly by a pike on the face and thigh, slightly by a cutlass on the shoulders, and after the surrender was knocked down by a four pound rammer, the blow of which was unfortunately near upon the same place, where the cutlass hit. You will do me a most singular favour to excuse the sally I took in the barge, and have me exchanged as soon as possible.

Yours affectionately, J. Cropper, Jnr.[169]

The British tossed most of the casualties overboard except for Commodore Whaley, whose corpse was recovered. Unsure of the fate of the Patriot troops, Colonel Cropper sought terms with Captain John Kidd. Cropper offered to transport the wounded from both sides of the conflict to receive medical treatment if Kidd would grant the colonial troops a reprieve. Kidd considered the terms and agreed if Cropper would release the men captured from his vessel, the *Jolly Tar*, which was captured on November 15.[170] The terms were considered mutually consensual, and the prisoners of both sides were released; Cropper took all of the wounded who sought treatment back to the mainland. Cropper was released on December 3, 1782, as was

Whaley's body (in order to be interred). On that day, Kidd wrote a letter to Cropper and confirmed he was releasing all of the prisoners and stated he was waiting for Cropper to do likewise of the men from the *Jolly Tar*. In a sense of civility, he concludes his letter: "We remain, Deer [*sic*] Sir, with Friendship, Yours."[171]

One report of Whaley's funeral states, "The remains of the brave Commodore Whaley were deposited by his comrades on the lonely beach of one of these islands, where they now rest, 'unhonored and unsung,' except by the 'sounding sea' as its waves break and moan upon the shore."[172] However, the consensus is that Commodore Whaley was carried by the Accomack County militia through Onancock and buried in the Corbin family plot at Scott Hall Cemetery on December 3, 1782, and given full military honors.[173] Solomon Evans, who had witnessed the battle perched in a tree on Smith Island, rounded up other islanders and gathered the floating bodies of sailors and buried them. The official marker for Commodore Whaley and all those who lost their lives during the Battle of the Barges is located at Scott Hall, and Whaley's individual gravesite marker is maintained by local residents even to this day to honor the man who gave his life to free his country.

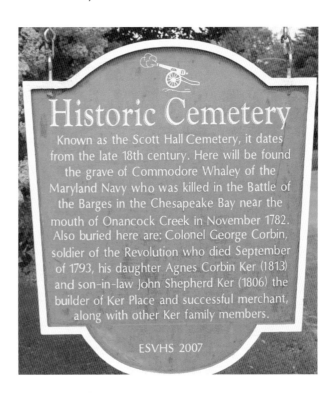

Scott Hall Cemetery.
Courtesy of the Eastern Shore of Virginia Historical Society.

The survivors of the Battle of the Barges, more properly known as the Battle of Cager's Straight (or Kedges Straits), were received as heroes by local Patriots. Despite the loss of the battle, it was viewed as an important part in the movement toward independence. Colonel Cropper returned home seriously wounded and bandaged but grateful to see his wife, Margaret "Peggy" Pettit, and their daughter, Sarah Corbin, safe and sound. He was elated to see his family and told them of his battle at sea, the swordfights that occurred, the explosion of the gunpowder and of his battle wounds. His wife responded, "You deserve it, a Continental officer [of the state *militia (emphasis added)*], to leave your wife and children to fight sailors on the water."[174] While she was glad to have her husband safe at home, she was certainly unmerciful with her rebuke of his decision to join the naval forces. Cropper was a decisive commander on the battlefield, but he never again countermanded orders received from the home front.

A few days later, Cropper's head wound reopened, so his wife decided to apply more stitches and fresh bandages. During the process, she was holding needles in her mouth and accidently swallowed one. Unfortunately, this choking accident resulted in the death of Margaret "Peggy" Pettit. The colonel and his young daughter were left devastated and alone. All of his servants had been abducted during the *Thistle* tender raid, and this left no one to care for his child, his household and his estate.

Colonel Cropper gave a harsh rebuke to the rest of the Maryland fleet that had sailed with them that fateful day. "There was never before on a like occasion so much cowardice exhibited," Cropper wrote to Maryland governor William Paca.[175] Captain Levin Handy confirmed this in a letter to the governor and stated that at the pre-battle strategy meeting, Commodore Whaley figured the enemy would focus on the *Protector* and ordered all of the other ships to support his flank and stern, and all of the officers agreed to do it or "all sink together."[176] He did confirm the accounts of Samuel Handy, Bryant, Frazier and Spedden that there was confusion or disobedience amongst the men of their vessels that caused them to not engage the enemy, but it was clear that Robert Dashiell had intentionally retreated. Because of his cowardice, on December 26, 1782, Captain Robert Dashiell was "cashiered" for "highly unbecoming and improper Conduct in the late Action with the Enemy."[177] Cashiering was not the same as a court martial; it did not go through the due process of a trial and did not carry criminal sentencing. During that time, most officers, when they were commissioned, invested or bonded their personal money into the purchase of weapons, uniforms, horses, ships, etc., with the expectation of being reimbursed at some point during or after the war. When a person was cashiered, he was immediately removed from his state-appointed commission, given a dishonorable discharge, had his insignia stripped (often in a humiliating public ceremony) and any bond or investment of the officer was forfeited to the government. This was the case of Robert Dashiell due to his retreat at the Battle of the Barges.

In a dreadful twist of irony, all of those men lost their lives the same day the initial Treaty of Peace was drafted by John Adams, Benjamin Franklin, John Jay and Henry Laurens of the United States and David Hartley and Richard Oswald of Great Britain.[178, 179] Many sailors on both sides of this battle had gruesomely lost their lives because a piece of paper had not yet been finalized.

Additional conflicts continued in the bay during February and March 1783, a time during which Governor William Paca informed George Washington that the British were not following the ceasefire order given by their commanders.[180] It was not until September 3, 1783, that the Treaty of Paris was officially ratified and Great Britain recognized the independence of the free and individual states of the United States of America. While this may have ended the war between Great Britain and the United States, it did not necessarily end the hostile emotions between the Patriot and Loyalist residents of the Eastern Shore.

PART SIX

MARMADUKE MISTER
AND STEPHEN MISTER

T o fully understand how the Mister family served on both sides of the Revolutionary War, the familial relationships themselves need to be examined. The Mister family's hypocritical background makes it rather difficult to believe they had true convictions toward either side of the war. For example, Levin Evans had been arrested in 1777 for piracy after he was mistaken for his relative Richard Evans (or so he claimed). Richard Evans was most likely a brother-in-law to Marmaduke Mister and married to Marmaduke's sister Judah or Judith (see Appendix D). An examination of this family results in a convoluted picture of what exactly was happening on the Eastern Shore during the course of the war.

There is insufficient evidence to give an exact date of arrival, but the Mister family arrived in America sometime prior to 1700, as shown in Appendices D and E. Marmaduke Mister the elder was born around 1660 and died some fifty years prior to the start of the Revolutionary War. He had a son, William Mister, who married Patience Harris. William and Patience gave birth to Abraham, William, Marmaduke, Judah, Sarah, Hannah, Isaiah and Patience. Residing in the Chesapeake Bay area meant that most of the family was involved in the fishing and sailing industries, but it is not known if piracy was part of the family's history.

Marmaduke Mister (the elder) patented a tract of land called Bachelor's Delight in Somerset County in 1683.[181] At that time, the land was still considered part of Somerset County, Maryland. It is known today to be part of the town of Laurel in Sussex County, Delaware.[182]

James Wyth, Marmaducke Mester pat[ent] 250 ac[res]

Charles C. [Charles Calvert, 3rd Baron Baltimore, 9th Proprietary-Governor of Maryland] *To all persons be whom those present shall come greeting in our Lord God Everlasting.*

Know Yee that whereas Col. William Stevens of Somersett County in one said province of Maryland has Due unto him two hundred and fifty Acres of land within our said province part of a warrant for four thousand acres of Land granted him the third day of May one Thousand six hundred Eighty Three and had Surveyed and Laid out for him a Tract of Land for two hundred and fifty Acres called Bachelor's Delight Lying in Somersett County.[183]

Land patent for Bachelor's Delight granted to James Wyeth and Marmaduke Mister on September 10, 1684, in Somerset County, Maryland.

Some authors have said that this tract of land was founded by pirates who sailed from the Chesapeake Bay with Captain John Cook and ventured on a voyage around the world. The pirates set sail in April 1683 and headed toward the west coast of Africa, arriving off of Guinea in November 1683.[184] They won the vessel, the *Bachelor's Delight*, from a group of Dutch sailors in a card game and continued their exploration around the world and eventually returned to Philadelphia; supposedly, some of those sailors bought this tract of land with booty they had confiscated.[185] However, this land patent was granted on May 3, 1683, as Bachelor's Delight, and it was sold to James Wyeth and Marmaduke Mister on September 10, 1684.[186] The actual pirates were well on their way toward Africa by May 3, so the legend of this property being patented by pirates from this expedition could not be accurate because the patent was granted before the pirates even crossed the Atlantic Ocean.

William's presumably eldest son, Abraham Mister, was the first of the brothers to profit from the Revolutionary War. On May 12, 1778, a correspondence to Governor Thomas Johnson authorized the auditor general to pay an amount due of over £133 for Mister's service of transporting colonial troops in his vessel on at least five separate occasions.[187] In today's dollars, that amount would be close to $30,000. There is no evidence within the records of the Maryland Militia that Abraham officially joined the Continental forces. This shows that one did not need to profess political convictions in order to gain a profit during the war. Abraham's younger brothers soon followed their older brother's entrepreneurial endeavors, though they did not necessarily directly profit from the colonial government.

Abraham's wife, Alice, gave birth to the infamous picaroon Stephen Mister. His father was already providing services to the Patriots by the time Stephen joined the war effort. It is most likely that Stephen was in his mid-twenties when he began his privateering enterprise upon the vessels and residents of the Chesapeake Bay. With that being known, it is remarkable how such a young man was able to command a force of brigands in the bay. Additionally, it is not exactly known how he colluded with his uncle, Marmaduke Mister, in order to plunder the bay for a number of years during the American Revolution.

William's second-oldest son, William Mister, was born about 1720. He married Comfort Evans on October 16, 1749, and she gave birth to sons William and Isaac. In some instances, literary works confuse William and Abraham because William had the middle name of Abraham. Therefore, some accounts list Stephen Mister as a child to William and Alice. However, three separate and distinct sons are listed on a Somerset County deed dated from 1762; it clearly states that Abraham and Alice, as well as William and Comfort, entered into a deed with Marmaduke Mister.[188] This evidence demonstrates that Stephen was the son of the elder brother, Abraham Mister. Regardless of his precise parentage, the important fact is that Stephen Mister was in close collusion with his uncle Marmaduke while privateering on the Chesapeake Bay.

William's third son, Marmaduke Mister, was born around 1722. Marmaduke's first marriage was to Rachel, who gave birth to Sarah, Naomy, Charity and Elizabeth. Rachel died around 1770, and Marmaduke married a woman named Sarah. They had two sons, William and Severn, who was born about 1785. Marmaduke gained a reputation as a ruthless pirate on the Chesapeake Bay and openly spoke out in favor of the Crown. In the years to come, his son Severn most likely benefited from his father's privateering operation and became a wealthy landowner and quite influential in the Chesapeake Bay region.

One of William's youngest children was a daughter by the name of Hannah Mister, who married John Evans on August 21, 1745. That family was blessed with numerous children, including Levin, Nathan, John, Abigail, Euphemia, William Mister, Jesse, Triphenia and Patience. Miraculously, Hannah managed to give birth to these nine children over the course of a twenty-year period. Levin Mister was born on February 27, 1744, and the last child, Patience, was born on April 15, 1765. It was dangerous for a woman to endure that many births across such a span of her life considering the conditions of the time and the isolation from medical treatment. Against the odds, the family persevered, and three of their sons went on to fight in the Revolutionary War.

Having recently emigrated from Great Britain, the Mister family probably had strong loyalties toward the British. This trait was shared by many other local families. During the war, Marmaduke Mister the younger and his brother's son, Stephen, worked as privateers for the British. Both of them were in cahoots and at times direct subordinates of the infamous picaroon Joseph Wheland; yet both Misters were well known for being ruthless pirates in their own right. They may have obtained official letters of marque to conduct such raids and confiscations, but in reality, the British fleet probably could not have cared less if the rogues actually went through proper official channels. Most likely, some of the plundering committed by both sides along the Eastern Shore was probably not officially sanctioned. The confiscation of goods could be a crime of opportunity combined with a lack of enforcement of justice.

The Misters, who were based out of Smith Island, captured Patriot boats and raided plantations along the bay. The area of Tangier Sound and Kedges Straits between the Annemessex River and the Nanticoke River became the favorite hunting grounds of Stephen Mister. The chief impetus of this endeavor was to hinder Patriot efforts and transfer useful vessels and arms to the British fleet. There were also other benefits to Mister, such as the loot confiscated from the enemy. However, not all of the rules of engagement were always followed by those on the Eastern Shore. Somehow, keeping the British pleased was secondary compared to running a lucrative family enterprise.

Stephen Mister was a threat in the Chesapeake Bay early in the Revolutionary War. He was arrested in September 1777 for high treason against the State of Virginia. On the fourteenth of that month, while in confinement in Baltimore County, he managed to escape from jail with the help of Reuben Warrington.[189] Mister was captured a year later, in November 1778, in Accomack County, Virginia, and was transferred to Worcester County, Maryland, to stand trial for high treason against that state, creating a temporary delay of his pirating practices.[190]

A letter sent to the Council of Maryland on March 30, 1779, identified Stephen Mister as a serious threat to the cause of liberty:

Sir,

We are informed by a Letter received to Day from Col° Hooper, that Meister and other of his Stamp have committed a Robbery on M° Arthur Whitely at his Plantation at Hooper's Streights; the Villains are supposed to have gone with their Plunder to Smith's Island. Col° Hooper proposes to send a Party of Militia after them; possibly he may want your Assistance to second the Operations of the Militia; if he should make such a Request, we wish you to give your Aid. Meister and his Gang are of the Sett who harbor in Armimessex [sic] and have plundered several Vessels as well as committed other Outrages.
Commodore Grason[191]

During the summer of 1780, Stephen Mister managed to capture at least six or seven vessels from the Tangier Sound and blockaded trade at the mouth of the Nanticoke River on the Chesapeake Bay. The following accounts all coincide with the early summer of 1780, presumably after Mister's confiscation of the ships from the sound. The court record indicates that Stephen Mister was tried on May 6, 1780, in Accomack County for treason against the state.[192] He was found guilty, and the justice ordered that he be sent to Richmond to await trial at the state's general court for criminals. On June 13, 1780, Stephen Mister was scheduled to appear before the court in Richmond. A little while later, at the Accomack County Court, a bill of sale from Stephen Mister was presented by the petitioner James Taylor, who had purchased an item that was being disputed. The court ordered the bill of sale valid and to be recorded on July 28, 1780. It does not state what the item was, the sale amount or why it was being disputed. So it cannot be determined from the court record if it was real property, personal property or perhaps a vessel, maybe even stolen goods. It is known that Colonel John Cropper was present in the court for the transaction, but the court record just notes his presence and does not state if he had a part in the trial or if he was just a mere observer. It is probably more than a coincidence that Stephen Mister's legal proceedings expeditiously became known to the governors of Maryland and Virginia shortly after this interaction; perhaps it was because of Cropper's attendance in the courtroom that it was only a matter of days before the governors were corresponding about the malicious marauder.

On August 3, 1780, Maryland governor Thomas Sim Lee sent the following dispatch to Virginia governor Thomas Jefferson:

> *Sir A certain Stephen Mister of the State of Virginia, stands indicted in the General Court of this State, for High Treason committed within this State: He was committed to the Goal* [sic] *of Baltimore County from whence he escaped. Soon after which, he was apprehended in Virginia and delivered to the Sheriff of Worcester County, to be returned to Baltimore, but he again made his Escape. I am informed he is now confined at Richmond to take his Trial at the approaching Court, for Treason against the State of Virginia, and that it is apprehended the Testimony will be incomplete from the Absences of Witnesses. Should he be acquitted from the Insufficiency of Evidence, I must solicit your Excellency to direct the Delivery of him to an Officer of this State for the Purpose of being tried for the Offence perpetrated against the State of Maryland and to that End I have enclosed your Excellency a Transcript of the Record under Seal.*[193]

Thomas Jefferson replied to Governor Lee from Richmond, Virginia, on August 15, 1780.

The following is the transcript of the reply:

On receipt of you Letter yesterday on the subject of Stephen Mister, I enquired of the Jailer and had from him information that such a person was Sent here from Accomack in June last, charged with high treason: that the Judges at the last court admitted him to bail, (the testimony probably appearing slight) binding him in a penalty of £100,000 himself and two sureties in £50,000 each for his appearance at the court in october next. Should he be cleared on trial I will see that due attention be paid to your Letter. In the mean time it will perhaps be best to say nothing as it might prevent his coming in.

I have the honor to be with every sentiment of esteem and respect, your Excellency's most obedient servant,

Tho. Jefferson[194]

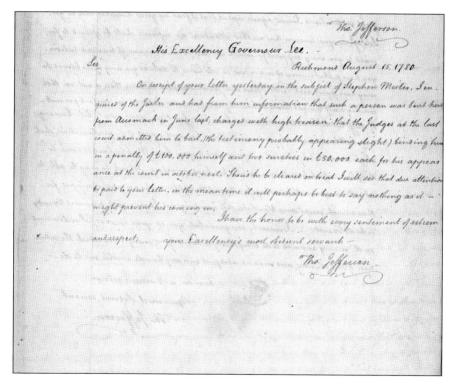

A letter from Thomas Jefferson to Governor Thomas Sim Lee of Maryland, 1780. *Image used by permission/courtesy of the British Library, MS 38650 A.*

In August 1780, after the arrest of Stephen Mister, Marmaduke Mister had a change of loyalties—or, more likely, a change of purse strings. Not only did Marmaduke Mister enlist into the service of the colonial militia, but three of his nephews did as well. The evidence shows that Marmaduke Mister enlisted into the Little Annemessex Company of the Princess Anne Battalion of the Maryland Militia in addition to his sister Hannah's sons William, Jesse and Levin.[195]

The only person existing at this time by the name of Marmaduke Mister was the Loyalist privateer from Smith Island. His grandfather, the only other Marmaduke Mister, had died much earlier. In 1780, Marmaduke would have been fifty-eight years old, which seems like an advanced age at which to engage in battle. However, even to this day, many residents of Smith Island live into their eighties or nineties, so for a fifty-year-old man to be sailing was not uncommon.

The Little Annemessex Company, commanded by Captain Henry Miles, was based out of the area of the Little Annemessex River around Crisfield, Maryland. It was part of Colonel Thomas Hayward's Princess Anne Battalion, which, like many Eastern Shore militia companies, did not see much action and seldom ventured beyond the border of their county.

The reason Marmaduke changed sides during the course of the war is not evident in the historical record, but there are some obvious conclusions. First, with the arrest and imprisonment of his nephew Stephen, Marmaduke's own freedom was at risk, and not wanting to face criminal charges, he might have decided to swear an oath of allegiance to fight with the Patriot forces. Secondly, Marmaduke had been receiving the captured loot from homesteads and vessels ransacked by Stephen. He might not have been able to support his family without a steady supply of the fenced booty. Finally, it is also likely that the privateer realized that the course of the war was shifting and decided to side with the most probable (or most profitable) victor. Whatever the reason, the Mister family became part of the Patriot side of the war in 1780. This change in allegiance did not stop privateers in the Chesapeake Bay, including Stephen Mister.

Marmaduke Mister and Richard Evans were registered in the Little Annemessex Company of the Princess Anne Battalion of Somerset County, Maryland Militia, 1780, and are listed as the eighteenth and nineteenth names in the right column (detail shown in inset on opposite page).

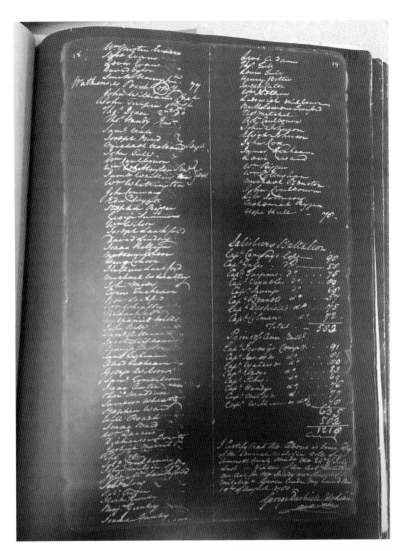

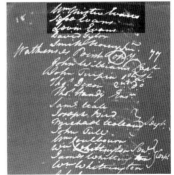

William Mister Evans, Jesse Evans and Levin Evans appear as the first three names in the left column (detail shown at right) in the muster roll of the Little Annemessex Company of the Princess Anne Battalion of Somerset County, Maryland Militia, 1780.

Stephen Mister was not dissuaded to stop his piracy against American vessels and farms. He continued his privateering ways and soon again made himself known to colonial officials. On June 27, 1781, the Maryland Council of Safety received this dispatch:

> *Whereas this Board have good reason to believe that…Stephen Mister… Somerset have been trading with the Enemy and that they are disaffected and Dangerous Persons whose going at large may be prejudicial to the State. The Lieutenants of Somerset and Worcester Counties are therefore ordered to arrest the persons above mentioned without delay and have them before the Board forthwith that they may be dealt with according to Law.*[196]

Even while Stephen Mister had returned to the bay to pillage the colonial fleet, his uncle Marmaduke Mister was sailing for Maryland, and there is evidence that Marmaduke fulfilled his duty to the colonial militia. His specific actions or role were somehow related to a naval capacity, and there is one confirmed account that he performed services for the new government. On November 22, 1781, the Maryland Council of Safety sent a notification that granted Marmaduke Mister safe passage to return to Maryland. "Marmaduke Mister has permission to return home by the 15 Inst, he having brought some American Prisoners from Tangier Island."[197] For this service, he received nine pounds from the council.[198] This might not be a significant account of his role, but it does assure that by the end of the Revolutionary War, Marmaduke Mister was fighting on the side of the Patriots.

As far as Marmaduke's personal finances, it seems that he was well-positioned in terms of property. It is known by a 1783 land assessment that he owned a one-hundred-acre property called Pitchcraft located on Smith Island along the Maryland-Virginia border.[199] The original tract of Pitchcraft consisted of one thousand acres surveyed in 1682 and was bound on three sides by bodies of water. This location would have allowed ample access for raiders to transport stolen goods to the island and hide amongst the inlets and marshes. It also allowed for easy concealment and numerous routes of escape when approaching enemy vessels were spotted.

Since the property was located on the Virginia and Maryland border, it was also referred to as Mister's Thoroughfare. Marmaduke Mister said he had witnessed them measure the boundary with chains and ropes to determine the dividing line. He claimed that back in the day, someone had marked a line from a gum tree to a cedar post and placed stones to indicate the boundary between the two states. As time passed, the problem faced by the 1870 boundary commission was that the cedar post had decayed, the gum tree had died, Mister had been dead for over seventy years and the rocks themselves were said to have been starting to break apart:

DEPOSITION OF JOHNSON EVANS

I have heard of a stone at "The Barn" point many years ago, ever since I was a boy, but have never seen it. "The Barn" from the stone I have found in Misters thoroughfare…a stone on the East side of Smiths island, about three-quarters of a mile or a mile North of this house at Horse hammock, at which children…had been taken when young and one or more of them whipped, and one or more of them ducked, to make them remember it as a boundary stone; a boundary of what I don't know; whether of two states or two owners of land I don't know.[200]

It may have only been through these cruel and traumatic punishments to children that the demarcation was actually remembered.

Marmaduke eventually died sometime around April 1798, and he saw that his family was provided for in his estate. Marmaduke made out his will and signed it on October 10, 1796 (see Appendix B), and it was fulfilled on April 21, 1798. He directed that a third of his personal property be given to his wife, Sarah. Furthermore, he willed that Sarah have his land and marshes until his son Severn reached the age of twenty-one, at which time the land should be equally divided between his two sons, William and Severn. The remainder of his personal estate was to be given to any children who had not received any real property in an amount equal in value to the land, and then any remainder was to be divided equally amongst all of his children. This was a fair reckoning of how families settled these matters during this time period. The interesting fact is the unusually high amount of personal property. If the two sons each received fifty acres of the real property at Pitchcraft, then the four daughters would each receive an equal fifty acres of personal property after having subtracted a total of a third of his personal property bequeathed to his wife.

Sarah Mister, as it turned out, was just as cunning as her scallywag of a husband and wanted to be sure that she received her fair deal of the inheritance. On May 16, 1798, the widow Mister appeared before the Somerset County Court and quitted her claim granted to her by her late husband in his last will and testament, in lieu of which she chose to receive the dowry due to her for remarriage.[201] The practice of an allotment or dowry was common at the time, allowing for widows with underage children to remarry in order that there might be a head of the household. She had already been given a third of Marmaduke's personal assets, but in this cunning maneuver, she decided to give that up and claim her dowry. By claiming this right, the court treated the situation as if the deceased had died "intestate" (without a will). The dowry granted by law to Sarah Mister was not only a third of Marmaduke Mister's personal estate but also a third of his real estate. It seems as if Sarah may have learned a thing or two over the years from witnessing her husband's business arrangements.

Only William and Severn were Sarah's children; Marmaduke's other four children were from his first marriage to Rachel. The four children from the previous marriage were all female and most likely married. At the time, usually only male heirs inherited real estate property from their fathers. Sarah's motives for this legal action are not entirely clear—it is not known if Sarah did this to be selfish or if it was to be altruistic and give some property to the daughters. Will and property records would probably explain the full story, but that is not the focus of this work. The children's reception of this abrupt amendment to the will is not known, yet it appears that the sons still thrived off of the inheritance from their father.

Overall, the Mister family came out of the war fairly unscathed. In terms of property and personal wealth, the family did not face any significant losses. Marmaduke's widow and his children prospered from the family's privateering profits. In fact, his children were generally regarded as upstanding citizens and were highly respected within the community, but the family would face devastating personal losses in the next generation.

PART SEVEN

SEVERN MISTER AND THE REVEREND JOSHUA THOMAS

armaduke Mister's son Severn was born shortly after the conclusion of the Revolutionary War. Severn had strong Methodist religious convictions and, had he been of age, probably would have been a conscientious objector refusing to take up arms for either side of the conflict. In the years following the War of 1812, Severn started to make substantial land purchases throughout the bay. Eventually, he and his wife, Keziah, and their two small children, Hannah and Bennett, moved to nearby Deal Island. The move to Deal Island was followed by the birth of three additional sons, Richard, Lowder and David Mister. In the fishing industry, additional children meant more deckhands and more help in processing the fish and crabs that were caught. The births of the three boys brought quite a sense of fulfillment to the Mister family.

In 1814, Severn started to buy tracts of land and constructed a new home for his family, which still remains standing on the island today:

> Built during the first decades of the nineteenth century, [this] house is perhaps the oldest dwelling to survive on Deal Island. The two-story, hall-parlor house retains distinctive Federal style details common to the second quarter of the nineteenth century…Construction of this prominent frame house is attributed to Severn Mister, who started purchasing various tracts on Deal Island in 1814. Parts of "Purgatory," "Barbadoes," and "Self Preservation," were included in the $1,700 purchase from Thomas Rowe. Eight years later Mister bought an additional tract called, "Grave's End" from Charles Jones.[202]

The Severn Mister House. Maryland Historical Trust Determination of Eligibility Form compiled by Paul Touart, June 19, 1986, Somerset County Historical Trust, Princess Anne.

When he moved to Deal Island, Severn Mister was blessed by becoming close friends with the "Parson of the Islands." Before the Revolution, there had been a mass exodus of Anglican priests from the churches that existed on the peninsula. Likewise, with the numerous islands in the bay, it was not possible to have a minister on every island. At the time, most islands did not even have a church, so many Eastern Shore residents could not attend a weekly church service. This gave rise to new methods of worship, including the introduction of camp meetings and revivals, during which worshipers would travel to a certain location and everyone would celebrate together. Another method that arose involved an itinerant minister who would travel to multiple communities over the course of a set rotation. The most notable itinerant pastor in the Chesapeake Bay during this time was Reverend Joshua Thomas, who was so influential that he came to be affectionately known as the Parson of the Islands. Reverend James A. Massey once stated, "[I]t becomes a grateful, and a useful task to perpetuate the influence and example of a good life—such a life as that of Joshua Thomas."[203]

An engraving of Reverend Joshua Thomas, the Parson of the Islands, marked by Van Ingen and Snyder and printed in *The Parson of the Islands: The Life and Times of Joshua Thomas*, by Adam Wallace, 1861.

Thomas began his preaching career around 1805 as a Methodist minister, but he was not always known for that position. He was actually raised as a waterman and sailed the bay and was focused on becoming a family man. Early in life, he had a love for music and dance and married when he was twenty-three. As a sailor, he started transporting people between the islands to attend camp meetings and revivals but was just a bystander and did not participate in the religious gatherings even though he had been known to read his prayer book regularly. As if by a miracle, one day he started to preach aloud while attending a meeting, and the people gathered around him. This transformed him, and after that, he became the Parson of the Islands. He traveled to most of the islands along the Eastern Shore in a wooden, hand-hewn canoe called the *Methodist*.[204] The canoe had a length of about thirty feet and a breadth of five feet. The tree that it was carved from was so massive that when it was cut down, it shook the ground for miles around, and people thought there was an explosion of cannon fire.[205] The tree was reportedly so large that it produced two canoes of this massive size.

Shortly after Thomas's epiphany, the War of 1812 once again placed the United States at odds with Great Britain. Because of its isolation, the Eastern Shore was somewhat surprised when Admiral Sir George Cockburn landed his fleet off Tangier Island. He declared the island's

Portrait of Admiral Sir George Cockburn by John James Halls depicting the burning of Washington, circa 1817. *Courtesy of the National Maritime Museum, Greenwich, London.*

residents prisoners of the Crown and proceeded to build forts there to make it his base of operations. The British started to deforest the island in order to erect the fortifications and housing for all of the soldiers. When the British were approaching the prayer grove where Thomas held his camp meetings, the reverend approached the admiral and pleaded for him to save the sacred grove. Admiral Cockburn knew the parson to be a pious man and took him at his word of honor. He assured Thomas that his men would not take a single tree from that site. Because of his respect for the parson and the lack of Anglican priests, the admiral actually allowed Thomas to be the chaplain for his troops and provide services for his men and the other island residents.[206]

Admiral Cockburn was the officer who later ordered his troops to burn Washington, D.C. They razed the U.S. Capitol and the Presidential Mansion (the White House), amongst several other governmental buildings as well as integral items of infrastructure. He even went as far as to demolish the newspaper *National Intelligencer* and ordered every "C" of typeset destroyed "so that the rascals can have no further means of abusing my name."[207]

Reverend Thomas found allies on Deal Island among Severn Mister and his family. The congregation on Deal Island had grown to such numbers that Thomas decided to make it his home base in about 1825. With his followers increasing in number, Thomas held the first Methodist camp meeting on Deal Island on July 17, 1828.[208] Severn Mister was one of the esteemed members of the board of managers for that first camp meeting. Even though Marmaduke Mister had died in 1798, his family allowed the preacher to hold services in his house on Smith Island for several years.[209] The Mister family created a close friendship with Reverend Thomas that would remain steadfast even through troubling hardships.

Living on a small island, one can imagine that there would be occasional neighborly disputes. During one such quarrel between Thomas and Severn Mister, the minister heard that Mister was about to set sail for Baltimore. Thomas rowed out to Mister's schooner, where it was under anchor. He came aboard the ship and wanted to reconcile their differences before Mister set sail. Mister rebuked Thomas, stating that he had not asked for permission to come aboard, and ordered him off the deck. The minister returned to his boat and waited in silence alongside Mister's schooner. Being in a cross mood that morning, Mister eventually came over and asked the reverend to disengage so that he may raise anchor:

Brother Thomas replied, "I cannot leave you in this way, brother; you are bound on a voyage, and something may occur to prevent your return. This is an uncertain world, and yours is an uncertain life! What if you should go to the bottom, and to the bar of your God in the spirit you now show, and with the feelings you bear against me. Would he justify you? Or suppose I am removed by death, before your return, and leave you with this malice in your heart to carry on with you to your grave! Is this right for neighbors, and Christians? Think a moment, dear brother."[210]

Mister hesitated only but a second before reaching out to help the reverend back onto the deck of the schooner. Tears began to flow down the captain's face, and the two knelt down together and prayed for forgiveness and a safe voyage for the captain. The two never again had a misunderstanding and remained close, intimate friends.

PART EIGHT

THE SALT POND

On December 1, 1839, Severn Mister purchased from David C. Taylor a property known as the Salt Pond, located in Northumberland County, Virginia, which was bound by Chesapeake Bay to the east, Ball Creek to the north and the salt pond to the south (see Appendix C). The plantation extended across a total of about 550 acres and consisted of cultivable land as well as a salt pond. With the salt riots of 1776, the presence of a source of salt was rather important to the region. However, with harvestable salt in the tidal pools around the Salt Pond, it was also imperative to determine the amount of land that was actually hospitable to the growth of crops. The parties extensively discussed the total amount of land, the amount of acreage that was sustainable and which crops could prosper. The land transactions that surrounded this property were somewhat suspicious.

The Salt Pond had been bought by David C. Taylor on October 15, 1839, for $8,300.[211] On December 1, 1839, with the ink barely dry from the previous sale, Mister purchased the Salt Pond from Taylor for the large sum of $12,000, which, in today's currency, would amount to almost $300,000. Certainly, Mister would have had access to the land record that would show he was offering almost $4,000 more than what Taylor paid a month and a half earlier for the property, which creates the question why he would pay that much more for the tract. The land's worth, estimated in today's value, would be quite a sizeable sum for that many acres. It is hard to be precise, because several of the acres of the northeasternmost part of the property, where Ball Creek flows into the Chesapeake Bay, are now underwater.

Mister purchased the land for this exorbitant sum, and it is not clear how he obtained the financing. It was most likely not funded by his personal bank account. Severn's mother, Sarah, had claimed a third of Pitchcraft, the one-hundred-acre estate that belonged to Marmaduke Mister (Severn's father) when he died, leaving approximately sixty-six acres to be divided between Severn and his brother, William. Additionally, Severn's previous property on Deal Island was transferred to the ownership of his son, Bennett Mister, in November 1839.[212] If the money did not come from his inheritance or the sale of his real estate on Deal Island, could it possibly have been funded by caches of pirated loot that had been confiscated and collected through his family's privateering practices? The amount used to purchase the land was quite extraordinary, and there is no known logical explanation as to how Severn funded the purchase.

Severn Mister had relocated to the Salt Pond in 1839, but by September 1842, he decided to divide and sell the property to two other men. In order to make this sale, Mister needed to determine the boundaries of the newly divided lots, which was absolutely necessary when subdividing a parcel of land. On August 4, 1842, Robert Alexander conducted an extensive and thorough survey of Mister's land and informed the owner of the boundaries of his 477 acres of land. The official survey conducted by Robert Alexander determined:

> *Plat of the 'Salt Pond' tract of land surveyed for Capt. Severn Mister Aug. 4th, 1842, beginning at a cross ditch at A, and moving up the neck road… to a corner at B, Thence with Tho. E Harding's line…to a stump,… (passing two oaks)…to a locust…to the head of Ball's Creek at C, Thence with the meander thereof to its mouth, and along the Bay Shore and up another small creek to a corner with Tho. W Hughlott at D, Thence with his line, (in a ditch)…to a corner in the road at E, thence up the road…to the beginning—which said lines and boundaries enclose Four hundred and seventy seven acres of land.*[213]

There appeared to be a significant discrepancy between the land survey and the "550 acres" that Mister had purchased from Taylor. Considering the vast sum of money he had paid, Mister confronted Taylor about the discrepancy, and in his defense, Taylor claimed that an exact figure had never been stated, but rather that they had discussed the amount of arable land and what types of crops could be produced. Within a short period of time, the two became involved in a prolonged legal dispute about the

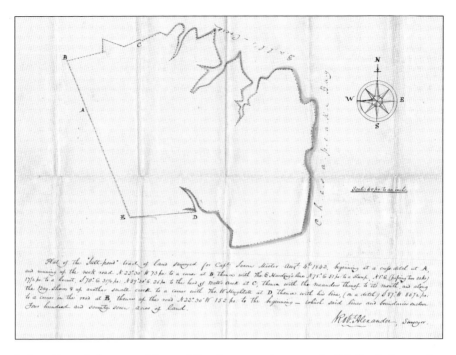

Robert Alexander's survey of Severn Mister's property known as the Salt Pond. *Courtesy of the Library of Virginia.*

land sale. Even with this legal battle ensuing, on September 22, 1842, Mister managed to sell the land (which is now known as Hughlett's Neck) to two buyers for a combined sum of $10,400.[214] Even though he suffered a financial loss in this sale, Mister did not disparage, because the Parson of the Islands, Reverend Joshua Thomas, happened to have been present when Mister and Taylor discussed the terms of the negotiation, and he could testify on behalf of Mister.

Mister sent a dispatch to Thomas, his longtime friend, asking him to testify to the property transaction. Of course the reverend agreed, and Mister said he would send a vessel on an appointed day to transport the minister. On that day, no such vessel arrived, and the reverend became concerned because he did not want to renege on his promise to his faithful friend. With such important litigation hanging in the balance, Thomas sought another vessel that might transport him across the bay.

Thomas came across a retired sea captain, "Captain P.," who had not sailed for some time, yet he had a schooner in the harbor fit to sail. He told the captain of his vow to testify for Mister and that he must set sail the following day in order to make it to the trial. The old man was bemused and said that due to his rheumatoid arthritis, he could barely make it back to his house—let alone sail across the Chesapeake Bay.[215] Thomas implored the old man that he needed to keep his promise and asked him: If God cured him, would he help him sail the next morning? The old man was skeptical but agreed that if he was cured, he would take the reverend wherever he wished.

By now, a few people had gathered around the men talking along the roadside, and they scoffed at the minister, claiming that the days of miracles had long since vanished. Nevertheless, the minister fell to his knees and began praying:

> *Here is our poor Brother, with a severe backache, and he has suffered considerably from his pains. I have no other prospect of fulfilling my promise, as thou knowest, but in his immediate recovery. I believe in thy great power. I trust in thy good providence. Thou wilt not suffer me to violate my word, or fail to help in this time of need. Now grant to cure this thy crippled servant that he may take me across the bay Lord! Thou art able; do the work, and I will go home and make ready to leave in the morning. Amen!*[216]

He urged the old sea captain to return home and to be ready at first light. The crowd dispersed, and all present, including the old captain, were incredulous about what they had just witnessed.

Early the next morning, the captain arose and found that his arthritic pain was gone. He quickly woke his wife, who had no knowledge of the previous day's events, and informed her that he was going to set sail. He urged her to get dressed and sail with him so that she might meet a most holy man. Not knowing the circumstances, she hastily got ready, and the couple went down to the pier. When they got to the landing, the parson was not present, so the captain went to the schooner to prepare to lay sail; there, he found the reverend already on board with his bag. The captain inquired as to how the parson knew that the old man was going to emerge from his house that morning. Thomas replied, "*I* knew you would be well, and now *you* see what God can do [emphasis added]."[217]

The schooner soon set sail across the bay and headed for Northumberland County. The seas were rough, because there was still a sharp wind left from a gale that had blown through the previous day. In fact, March 1843 saw one of the worst arctic plunge storms of that century, with temperatures twenty-five degrees below average for the mid-Atlantic states.[218] One particular storm that blew through in the middle of March dropped thirteen inches of snow in Washington, D.C., and twelve inches in Baltimore in a matter of twenty-four hours.[219] These sailing conditions were less than ideal and were downright dangerous. Despite the tumultuous weather, the parson and the captain set out to sail across the bay to the mainland of Virginia.

Thomas warned the captain to use caution—not just based on the weather conditions but because the reverend had a dire dream the night before:

> I had a strange dream last night brother, and it makes me fear some trouble ahead. I dreamed that I was upset in the water, and was trying to scramble up on a vessel's bottom, and that others were in distress around me. So, be careful.[220]

The minister's vision was alarming to the old sea captain, who was already not in the best of health. Reverend Joshua Thomas assured him to rest his worries and that they were safe in God's hands, but something close at hand was going to happen.

Thomas was correct that the schooner had safe passage to the Western Shore of Chesapeake Bay. Severn Mister was glad to see his friend Reverend Thomas, and he let the reverend know that the trial would convene the next day but asked why he had not traveled the day before in the ship that he had sent to transport him. The parson said that no such ship had arrived at the island the previous day. Mister informed him that he had sent his three youngest sons on a ship to fetch the minister in order to make it in time for the trial. At that moment, the reverend recalled his frightening dream and the blowing gale that had occurred the previous day. Not wanting to alarm his friend, he did not mention this to Severn Mister. However, Mister expected the worse, "My sons! my sons! my noble boys are lost!—They are gone! gone!"[221] Thomas went to the family's home to pray and tried to console them, urging them to not give up hope. No sign of Mister's ship or word from the young lads could be confirmed.

In regards to the legal proceedings surrounding the Salt Pond, Thomas swore his deposition before the court on March 15, 1843. Thomas, who had happened to be present when Mister and Taylor were discussing the terms of the land agreement, testified that:

> I told Capt. Mister I liked the plantation and then I axed Capt. Mister if
> he was able to give that much money for it without going debt, he told me

he was able, & well says I if you intend leaving Deal's Island, well then I told him I had rather for him to buy that plantation than any I had ever seen, then Capt. Mister observed that Twelve Thousand Dollars was too much to pay for Five hundred Acres of land. & then Capt. Taylor told him that there was Five hundred Fifty Acres or more...

Ques. by name. Did you distinctly hear David C Taylor assure Capt. Mister that the tract contained 550 acres of land

Ans. I understand him to best understanding to say it was that or more he never said less that.[222]

It was not only the Parson of the Islands's testimony that helped Mister win the lawsuit but that of several other individuals who testified to Taylor's assertions made during the land sale. The testimony of Reverend Thomas, combined with Robert Alexander's official land survey, certainly formed a solid foundation that helped determine the outcome of the case. On March 24, 1844, the court decided in favor of Mister and granted that $2,000 in

The Parson of the Islands, Accomack County, Virginia. *Courtesy of the Virginia Department of Historic Resources.*

restitution be paid to him by David Taylor, but this result did not offer the sorrowful Mister any satisfaction, as his three sons were still missing.[223]

The task of searching for Severn's missing vessel and sons continued for weeks. The family hoped the boys might have been able to escape the winter storm and sought refuge in a cove or inlet, or perhaps the fierce and rolling waves forced them out to open sea, yet the search was in vain. A few weeks later, the first body was found. Shortly thereafter, the second son was discovered, and immediately following, Reverend Joshua Thomas and another circuit preacher came across the body of the third as they were leaving a service at Holland Island.[224] All three boys had drowned during the storm, and their vessel was never found. The three had died while they were in their early twenties, before they could even start families of their own. Being in grief himself, Reverend Thomas recused himself from the funeral proceedings, and the Reverend Vaughan Smith gave the funeral service for the three boys.[225]

Joshua Thomas lived to be seventy-seven years old. He is buried on Deal Island at St. John's Methodist Episcopal Church, which is the oldest continuous Methodist meeting place in Somerset County. People still come there to pray at the Joshua Thomas Chapel and to visit his gravesite in the cemetery, where his marker gives a grim reminder of his preaching:

> *Come all my friends, as you pass by,*
> *Behold the place where I do lie*
> *As you are now, so once was I,*
> *Remember, you are born to die.*[226]

The events of Severn Mister's life were tumultuous. On one hand, he was prosperous when it came to personal wealth and property ownership. He was able to afford an estate that most people considered well beyond his means. While the land itself was not what was promised, his good friend the Parson of the Islands helped secure a lawsuit in his favor to recover his losses. However, this came at the price of the lives of his three youngest sons. Severn Mister died on December 30, 1855, and was buried in Royal Oak Cemetery in Talbot County, Maryland. It is hard to determine the overall success or failure of the Mister family's adventures upon the Chesapeake Bay, but it is certain that they are forever entwined in its history.

CONCLUSION

Without a doubt, the Eastern Shore of the Delmarva Peninsula was bestrewn with Loyalist sentiments throughout the Revolutionary War. In a letter sent to Maryland's first governor, Thomas Johnson, the militia commanders of Dorchester, Worcester and Somerset Counties affirmed that about 75 percent of their troops were Loyalists at heart.[227] The most contested issue with creating a new government was the ability for it to assert itself as the sovereign power. One of the people's greatest disagreements with the policies of the new government was the retention of landownership qualifications for voting rights. Many people thought one of the reasons for the rebellion was to obtain an equality of suffrage. However, the new government created limitations just as staunch as those that had previously existed. Other apparent justifications for why the transition to a new government was objectionable were not just political but included other reasons such as social and religious affiliations and economic factors. The isolation of the islanders and the Eastern Shore families made the residents wary of any new changes happening on the mainland.

It is known that the Loyalist privateers of Chesapeake Bay disrupted shipping and trade, and whatever plunder they did not surrender to the British, they kept as bounty. The most notorious brigand of the bunch was Joseph Wheland, followed by some of the Mister family of Somerset County, Maryland. Between Wheland and the Misters, it was hard for Patriot forces to maintain a consistent source of supplies and information. Wheland himself was arrested in July 1776, and despite his pleas, the court refused to summon witnesses in his defense or provide him with due process of law. He was imprisoned for a few years without the court ever hearing the testimony of his witnesses.

Likewise, local merchants, farmers and seamen were unable to sustain a source of trade in order to provide enough income to support their families. The production of some of the most important goods, such as tobacco and salt, was disrupted. Families of the area not only relied on these commodities for personal use but also for income. These families were dealt a double blow by the fact that not only were their goods being confiscated but also exports to Great Britain were being restricted.

Another major transition during this time period was a religious reformation on the Eastern Shore. For several years, the presence of English Anglican priests had been steadily declining, while simultaneously, there was a rise of the more pacifistic religion of Methodism. On one hand, Anglicanism demanded an oath of allegiance to the British Crown, who was the head of the Anglican Church. This made it difficult for Anglicans to turn from their faith and join the Patriot movement. Likewise, Methodism did not believe in taking up arms, so those followers were compelled to not join either side of the fight. While religion may not have played a significant role in the overall outcome of the war, for this region, it was possibly a pivotal factor in the resistance to the war effort. General William Smallwood made this observation about religious conscientious objection:

> *Religion was the original cause of those Events, yet this urged as the Principal motive in every Instance, tho [sic] there are some Exceptions wherein Ignorant men from their Religious Attachments have been deluded (those are readily distinguished & to be pitied) yet by far the greater number conceal their true motives, & make Religion a Cloak for their nefarious Designs.*[228]

Both sides of the war effort granted letters of marque to sailors in order to confiscate goods from the enemy and gather intelligence on the movements of opposing forces. For the most part, the privateers of the bay enjoyed the luxury of plundering and pillaging without having to fight in actual battles. Rather, the British privateers were present to hinder the war-making efforts of the state governments and militias and to disrupt the flow of commerce and communication. A letter written to General George Weedon on June 19, 1781, states:

I am convinced…to the latter their boats are frequently seen to pass and repass, the inhabitants in general disaffected – You have (I don't doubt) heard of the enemy plundering [the Tories as well].[229]

Captain John Greenwood might have summarized it best when he stated that the privateers

in general were a set of gallows-marked rascals, fit for nothing but thieves; hell-hounds and plunders from the inoffensive, unarmed people… without any kind of principle and I really believe that ten honest, religious, determined men could intimidate…a hundred such villains. Their whole object was plunder and they paid no…regard to the vessel they despoiled, be it loyal or otherwise; gain was all they sought, and to acquire from others what they were through mere laziness unable to obtain for themselves.[230]

The British enlisted privateers to monitor the sea and shores of the Chesapeake Bay, yet they were reluctant to recruit infantry from amongst the Eastern Shore residents. With a notable Tory presence in the bay, it is not immediately clear why the British did not utilize the Loyalists living there in order to launch an attack on the mainland:

If the British or Loyalist surrogates could have separated Maryland's Eastern Shore from the Patriot movement by cutting off the flow of supplies and restricting communications that crossed the region, they might have improved their chances in suppressing the rebellion.[231]

In order to prevent this, on May 1, 1781, the Maryland General Assembly passed the Act for the Defence of the Bay, which ordered the evacuation of all of the islands of Chesapeake Bay south of Hooper's Strait. The residents were permitted to remove all of their belongings other than any watercraft, which would be confiscated by the colonial militia and navy. Before this order could be enacted, British forces occupied an island in Holland Strait and prevented the implementation of the edict anywhere south of the Tangier Sound.[232]

When Lord Cornwallis surrendered at Yorktown on October 19, 1781, most Americans thought the war was over. Despite his surrender and the presence of the French navy, the devastating Battle of the Barges in the Chesapeake Bay was still to come. The battle that occurred in November 1782 was substantial in the sense that whichever side controlled the Chesapeake

Bay would control the trade of the colonies; the defeat at Yorktown would be inconsequential if the British gained control of the flow of trade. This is why the Battle of the Barges was such a crucial point in the war, albeit one that seems to be frequently glossed over in history textbooks. If the bay had continued to be blockaded, international trade and timely communication amongst the colonies would have been almost impossible.

The Maryland Council had ordered Commodore Zedekiah Whaley to engage the British in September 1782. The outcome of the Battle of the Barges could have been significantly different if the council would have waited for the arrival of French reinforcements. But due to the sense of urgency, the statesmen ordered the commodore to proceed and engage the British force. Even though his reinforcements had not yet arrived, his gear had not been properly stowed and it went against his better judgement, Commodore Whaley set sail. This one decision may have been the cause of the defeat that befell his fleet. Despite a devastating and deadly accident during this battle, America was still able to maintain control of this vital waterway.

Furthermore, Colonel John Cropper, who was severely wounded during the battle, not only provided medical treatment for his men but also for all of Commodore Kidd's British Loyalists. In a petition made to the state auditor, Cropper stated "that in addition to the calamities of war and cruelties exercised; the plundering of our property, and the burning of our habitations, so successfully and so wantonly practiced by the British Barges on this shore, we had to struggle with and to combat the secret machinations of internal enemies, more dangerous, if possible, than those open and avowed ones."[233]

Although Colonel Cropper was opposed to the Loyalist fighters, he made a claim to the auditor for about £190 that he had personally paid for the care of Kidd's wounded men. Cropper was not the only one who felt the internal threat of those on the Eastern Shore. Joseph Dashiell also commented to Governor Thomas Sim Lee, "I consider them [the people of the islands] the most dangerous enemy we have to watch."[234]

The conflicts that followed the surrender at Yorktown occurred on more localized terrain (as opposed to that of a national campaign). These engagements potentially had more importance to the bay residents than the overall Revolutionary War itself. Both sides were at the point of negotiating final terms of surrender. With the war ending, colonial privateers no longer had lucrative contracts to confiscate goods and property. Additionally, local colonists were unsure about whether or not they would receive compensation for goods confiscated—by either side—during the war. Fortunately, the skirmishes that followed were short-lived, and the war did come to a complete end with the signing of the Treaty of Paris on September 3, 1783.

In the aftermath of the Revolution, George Washington was confronted with the perplexing problem of whether or not to impose a punishment upon his own countrymen who had fought against the Patriot movement. It was a problem that the early leaders of the country debated, but it did not take long to come to a consensus. Washington did not want to place harsh penalties upon those Loyalists who wished to remain in the newly formed country. The civil authorities paroled most prisoners who had been incarcerated for treason; some chose to return to Great Britain, while other British sailors sought refuge within the new American colonies and others just resumed their lives in their local communities with their families.

Pirates like Joseph Wheland and a few members of the Mister family remained some of the most nefarious privateers at large. In reality, within the Mister family, only Richard Evans, Stephen Mister and Marmaduke Mister were known to serve as pirates or privateers for the British. These names soon disappeared from the minds of officials as they focused on forming a new government. In contrast, Abraham Mister provided services for the Patriots, and Jesse, Levin and William Evans served in the Maryland Militia. In a twist of fate, even Marmaduke Mister eventually joined that same militia. The Mister family's sailing prestige would be called into question after the drownings of Richard, Lowder and David Mister during the epic winter gale of March 1843. Severn Mister could not find solace after the loss of his children and most likely questioned his fateful decision—sending his sons to transport Reverend Joshua Thomas to testify in the Salt Pond case—for the rest of his life.

The Loyalist movement ultimately failed despite its widespread presence in the region of the Eastern Shore of Maryland and Virginia. It is estimated that the majority of Eastern Shore residents were sympathetic to the Loyalist movement. Ultimately, the Americans may have defeated the British in the Revolutionary War, but this did not necessarily dispel the resentment of Eastern Shore residents toward mainlanders. The most probable cause of the Loyalist downfall was a disorganized sense of local leadership. The British government scoffed at the idea that local militias could help the British infantry. Had this been done, the local Loyalists most assuredly could have provided reconnaissance for the British in monitoring the region. If the Tories could have maintained a coordinated attack to create a sustained presence, they might have been able to contain the local state militia units or perhaps even taken the Maryland and Virginia mainland. Overall, the British government's distrust of the local colonial residents proved to be a contributing factor in the loss of their control of the American colonies.

A secondary cause of the ineffectiveness of the naval war in the Chesapeake Bay was the design of the vessels themselves. The British and French obviously had used seafaring vessels in order to make the journey across the Atlantic Ocean. The most famous ships were the British man-of-war and the French frigate. They were large, heavily armed vessels and carried supplies for long journeys. In contrast, the local ships and barges in the bay were much better equipped for rivers and inlets. Schooners were capable of high speed and agility and were able to outrun other vessels. Likewise, barges were shallow-draft vessels, and their construction allowed them to sail into inlets and marshes, where larger vessels could not enter. This maneuverability, combined with the crews' knowledge of the local waterways, made it nearly impossible for the British or French naval fleets to pursue the local ships and barges without facing the calamity of running aground or being ambushed.

The emotions, convictions and fear felt by the residents in this region during the war must have been intense. The justifications for their actions were numerous and ranged from patriotism to self-defense to pure profit. Great Britain had an opportunity to maintain control of this region, but their skepticism of the local forces made them reject the idea of including the colonists as a major part of their war solution. After the war was over, many residents were still doubtful of the new government and held personal loyalties to the British government. Even to this day, the isolation of the Eastern Shore and the islands of Chesapeake Bay set them apart as their own unique communities locked away in the vault of time.

GLOSSARY OF COMMANDERS AND VESSELS

Author's note: The British leaders are preceded by their title and then alphabetized by their titular domain and not necessarily by their birth last name.

BRITISH-LOYALIST FORCES

Commanders

Sir Cockburn, Admiral George, 10th Baronet (April 22, 1772–August 19, 1853): The admiral sailed his fleet to Tangier Island during the War of 1812. He allowed the minister Joshua Thomas to act as the chaplain for his troops. He is best known for the burning of Washington, D.C., on August 24, 1814. Cockburn was eventually appointed the Admiral of the Fleet and also First Naval Lord.

Lord Cornwallis, Charles, the 1st Marquess Cornwallis (December 31, 1738–October 5, 1805): Cornwallis served as a commanding general during the American Revolution and is most known for his surrender to George Washington at the Battle of Yorktown on October 19, 1781. Although his surrender brought an end to the major engagements, it did not officially end the war. Despite his surrender, he was made a knight in the Order of the Garter and went on to serve as the Governor-General of India.

Lord Dunmore, John Murray, the 4th Earl of Dunmore (1730–February 25, 1809): Murray, more commonly referred to by his noble title, Dunmore, was a Scottish peer and served as the governor of the Province of New York and succeeded the Governor of the Colony of Virginia to become the last Royal Governor of Virginia at the start of the Revolution. He also planned many of the movements of the Royal Fleet in the Chesapeake Bay. After the burning of Norfolk on New Year's Day in 1776, Dunmore realized that he could not regain control of Virginia and eventually returned to Great Britain, where he was later appointed as the governor of the Bahamas.

Evans, Captain Richard: This colonist fought as a privateer for the British fleet and was related by marriage to Captain Marmaduke Mister. He assisted Joseph Wheland by providing food and a vessel during the Yell and Mariman incident of July 1776. He enlisted with Mister in the Little Annemessex Company of the Maryland Militia in 1780.

Kidd, Captain John: He was a Loyalist who commanded six barges of escaped slaves and British "refugees" during the "Battle of Barges." Kidd, whose flagship was the *Kidnapper*, defeated Commodore Whaley and Colonel John Cropper on November 30, 1782.[235] Kidd was seriously wounded during this engagement, but survived.

Mister, Marmaduke (1722–1798): The younger Marmaduke Mister was the landowner of Pitchcraft on Smith Island and a privateer for the British fleet aboard a schooner. In 1780, he enlisted as a private in the Little Annemessex Company of the Maryland Militia. Marmaduke was an uncle to Stephen Mister and father of Severn Mister.

Mister, Captain Stephen: Captain Mister was a leading British privateer in the Chesapeake Bay and the nephew of Marmaduke Mister, who helped him sell captured goods and excess plunder.

O'Hara, General Charles (1740–February 25, 1802): He was the British general who officially surrendered to the Americans at Yorktown in 1781.

Wheland, Captain Joseph Jr. (1730–February 25, 1809): He served as the commanding officer of the British privateer vessels in the Chesapeake Bay. He also served as the pilot to Lord Dunmore's vessels, including the tender of his man-of-war.

Ships

Jolly Tar: The *Jolly Tar* was under the direction of Captain John Kidd but was captured on November 15, 1782, by Commodore Zedekiah Whaley. The British sailors were released in an exchange with Colonel John Cropper after his defeat at the Battle of the Barges.

Kidnapper: Captain John Kidd commanded this vessel during the November 30, 1782 Battle of the Barges. Kidd's men boarded the *Protector* and defeated Commodore Zedekiah Whaley and Colonel John Cropper.

Ladies Revenge: This British vessel was involved in the Battle of the Barges.

Otter: It was a ship commanded by Captain Matthew Squire, who sailed with Captain Joseph Wheland during some of his raiding missions.

Ranger: The *Ranger* was commanded by Captain Young, who was wounded during the Battle of the Barges.

Roebuck: This British warship helped provide artillery to Loyalist units that destroyed the Somerset County weapons arsenal in 1778.

Tender: It was a British man-of-war tender commanded by Captain Joseph Wheland and was used to seize other vessels throughout the Chesapeake Bay. (The term "tender" refers to a transport vessel or a supporting cargo ship. The actual vessel's name is not known.)

Thistle Tender: This was a small, rowed vessel that attacked Colonel Cropper's residence, Bowman's Folly, on February 12, 1779. This was most likely a tender to a vessel known as the *Thistle*, but the most contemporary ship in that region with that name was involved in the War of 1812.

AMERICAN-PATRIOT FORCES

Commanders

Bryan, Captain Daniel: Captain Bryan served aboard the *Flying Fish* and was under the command of army Captain John Lynn following the conclusion of the war.

Cropper, Lieutenant Colonel John (December 23, 1755–January 15, 1821): He assumed command of the *Protector* and the rest of the fleet after the death of Commodore Zedekiah Whaley. He fought in the Battle of Monmouth and the Battle of Brandywine. At Brandywine, he received a bayonet wound to his leg. When the flag bearer was shot, Cropper grabbed a musket ramrod and tied a piece of cloth to it and carried it as his regiment's flag. He later went on to fight in the War of 1812 and was eventually elevated to the rank of general. He also served in the Virginia House and Senate.

Dashiell, Colonel George: The colonel was in charge of the Somerset County (Maryland) Militia from Nanticoke and was a brother to Colonel Joseph Dashiell.

Dashiell, Colonel Joseph: He was a Whig and was the county lieutenant for Worcester County, Maryland, and a colonel in the Maryland Militia. He was a brother to Colonel George Dashiell.

Dashiell, Captain Robert: He was a member of the Maryland State Navy and was in command of the barge *Terrible*, and due to his retreat during the Battle of the Barges, he was cashiered out of the navy (i.e., essentially relieved of command but without a court martial punishment).

Delisle, Captain: The captain commanded the schooner *Venus* after it was commissioned during the Bay Defence Act of October 1780.

Fallin, Major Daniel: The major's men arrested Joseph Wheland in 1776 near Holland Strait after his crew had fallen ill from smallpox.

Frazier, Captain Solomon: He commanded the barge *Defence*, sailed around the Tangier Island region and was involved in the Battle of the Barges.

Greenwood, Captain John: His schooner was overtaken by Joseph Wheland in the fall of 1781. The boat was captured and put into tow, but Greenwood remained on board and was able to recapture the vessel from its captors.

Handy, First Lieutenant Joseph: Handy was a commanding officer aboard the barge *Protector*, and he had his arm blown off at the Battle of the Barges on November 30, 1782. He continued to fight until he ultimately lost his life in the battle.

Handy, Lieutenant (Captain) Samuel: He was in charge of the barge *Langodoc* during the Battle of the Barges on November 30, 1782.

Hayward, Colonel Thomas: Hayward was the colonel of the Princess Anne Battalion of the Somerset County Militia. In 1780, multiple members of the Mister family enlisted as privates into the Little Annemessex Company of Hayward's unit.

Hooper, Colonel Henry: He was the colonel of the Dorchester County (Maryland) Militia. In 1778, his troops responded to the destruction of the state's powder magazine by British forces. In 1779, he sent a letter to the Council of Maryland about the destruction being inflicted by Joseph Wheland. He also petitioned for the passage of the Act for the Protection of the Bay Trade in 1782.

Lincoln, General Benjamin (January 24, 1733–May 9, 1810): This general was the one who officially accepted the surrender of the British at the Battle of Yorktown.

Smallwood, General William (1732–February 14, 1792): He was the brigadier general of the 1st Maryland Infantry and apprehended the pirates Hamilton Callalo and Thomas Moore. He was also the person who mistakenly accused Levin Evans of being a pirate. In 1778, Congress ordered him to command Virginian infantry units as reinforcements to the Maryland forces. He succeeded William Paca as the governor of Maryland in 1785.

Snead, Major Smith: This man fought with Commodore Whaley and Colonel Cropper during the Battle of the Barges and was taken prisoner by Captain John Kidd.

Spedden, Captain Levin: Spedden commanded the barge *Fearnaught* during the Battle of the Barges on November 30, 1782.

Whaley, Commodore Zedekiah (?–November 30, 1782): He was from Worcester County, Maryland, and he commanded the American fleet in the southern Chesapeake Bay. He was killed in the Battle of the Barges, also known as the Battle of Cager's Strait, when his ship, the *Protector*, was boarded by Captain John Kidd's men of the British *Kidnapper*.

Woodford, General William (October 6, 1734–November 13, 1780): He was a brigadier general in the Virginian Militia that later became part of the Continental army. It was his attack at Norfolk that drove Lord Dunmore out of Virginia. He fought at the Battle of Brandywine with George Washington as well as at the Battle of Monmouth.

Ships

Alliance: This fifty-six-gun frigate of the Continental navy was commanded by Captain Peter Landais. The vessel transported the Marquis de Lafayette back to France in 1778.[236] Landais was relieved of command and replaced by Captain John Barry.

Defence: She was a Maryland State Navy barge that was led by Captain Solomon Frazier and was involved in the Battle of the Barges on November 30, 1782.

Dolphin: The ship was a Maryland State Navy sloop that carried a crew of ten men and an armament of two guns. It was mastered by Joseph Dashiell and owned by John Fassett and Co. of Worcester County, Maryland. The boat bonders were issued a letter of marque on August 6, 1778.[237] The sloop, based out of Worcester County, would most likely be the one involved in the events contained in this book based on the proximity of its location.

Enterprise: She was a Maryland State Navy brig that aided Colonel Henry Hooper in 1778 to respond to the destruction of the state's powder magazine by British forces.

Fearnaught: This barge was one of Commodore Whaley's lead vessels and was commanded by Captain Levin Spedden with Lieutenant Zadock Botfield. Whaley remained in port at Baltimore until September 28 waiting for the arrival of the *Fearnaught*. This was one of the main barges of the fleet that was involved in the Battle of the Barges. She was the supply ship for Commodore Whaley's fleet.

Flying Fish: This schooner conducted island and shoreline surveys and reconnaissance during the Battle of the Barges and was commanded by Captain Daniel Bryan.

Langodoc: This was a small barge captured from the British and placed under the command of Lieutenant Samuel Handy.

Protector: This vessel was commanded by Lieutenant Samuel Handy, who was later transferred to the *Langodoc*. During the Battle of the Barges, it was commanded by Commodore Whaley with Colonel Cropper as second-in-command.

Terrible: Captain Robert Dashiell commanded this barge, which retreated at the Battle of the Barges. Dashiell was later relieved of command.

Venus: This schooner was commanded by Captain Delisle. It was commissioned during the Bay Defence Act of 1780. It was given a letter of marque on July 5, 1781, and carried a crew of seventy and sixteen guns. The master was James Buchanan, and he was granted the bond of $20,000. The owner was listed as Archibald Buchanan.

Victory: It was a British barge that was captured by American forces. She was manned by Colonel Cropper's Accomack County Militia during the Battle of the Barges, but it ran aground and was not able to participate in the conflict.

MARMADUKE MISTER'S WILL

The following is the transcript of the will pictured on pages 114 and 115.

In the Name of God amen I Marmaduke Mister Somerset County in the State of Maryland…being in perfect strength of memory thanks be to God for it calling to mind the certainty of death being willing to settle my worldly estate making void all other will or wills by one made I ordain and listest this my last Will and Testament in form as following

Item. I give and bequeath my wife Sarah Mister the third part of all my estate. Item. I give my land and marsh to my wife Sarah Mister till my son Severn Mister comes to the years of twenty one then to be equally divided between my two sons William Mister and Severn Mister It is my desire that all my children that has not had anything yet, to be made up even with them that has had and then the remainder of my Estate to be equally divided amongst them all. I do ordain Solomon Evans my whole and sole Executor of this my last will and testament this tenth day of October one thousand seven hundred and ninety six –

Signed sealed and delivered in the presence of   Marmaduke Mister
Tests
William Thomas
Richard Evans X his mark
James Spencer X his mark

This page and opposite: Marmaduke Mister's will. Somerset County, Maryland, Somerset County Will Book, EB17 (Annapolis, MD: Maryland State Archives, 1796): 665–666. *Courtesy of the Collection of the Maryland State Archives.*

April the 21st day 1798 Then came Richard Evans & James Spencer of the subscribing witnesses to the within last will and Testament of Marmaduke Mister late of Somerset County deceased & swerally made oath on the holy Evangels of Almighty God that they did see the Testator within named sign & seal the within Will that they heard him publish pron. and declare the same to be his last Will & Testament and at the time of his so doing he was to the best of each of their apprehensions of sond [sic] disponing mind memory & understanding and that they did subscribe their names as witnesses to the same in the presence & at the request of the Testator and in the presence of each other. And they depose that they saw William Thomas subscribe his name as a witness to the same in the presence & at the request of the Testator Marmaduke Mister – Before Esme Baylay on the 16th day of May 1798 Then came Sarah Mister the Widow of Marmaduke Mister late of Somerset County deceased and quitted her claim to the several bequests and devises made to her in the will of the said husband deceased and elected in Lieu thereof her dowry or third part of the deceased estate, both real and personal-
Before Esme Bayly Reg.
Recorded in Liber EB No. 17 folio 665 & 666
Test. Esme Bayly Reg.

DEED TO THE SALT POND
BOUGHT BY SEVERN MISTER

The following is the transcript of the deed pictured on pages 118–120:

This Indenture made the first day of December in the year of Our Lord One Thousand Eight hundred and thirty nine between David C Taylor and Margaret S his wife of the County of Richmond and State of Virginia as the One part and Severn Mister Sen'. of the County of Northumberland and state aforesaid of the other part Witnesseth that the said David C. Taylor and Margarett S his wife for and in Consideration of the Sum of Twelve Thousand Dollars Current money of the United States to them in hand paid and secured to be paid at and before the sealing & delivery of these presents by the said Severn Mister Sen' the receipt whereof is hereby acknowledged. Have Given Granted bargained and sold enfeoffed conveyed released and Confirm and by these present do give grant bargain and sell enfeoff Convey Release and Confirm unto the said Severn Mister that his heirs and assigns forever All and singular that messuage tenement tract or parcel of land Situated in the County of Northumberland aforesaid in Hughletts Neck and bounded by the land of James Harding on the West On the South by the land of Thomas Hughlett on the east by the Chesapeake Bay and on the north by the land of Thomas Harding and containing by estimation about five hundred and fifty acres be the same more or less for the tract is sold for such quantity little or much as it contains which said tract of land was purchased by the said David C Taylor from William Harding as by the Deed from the said Harding to the said Taylor

This Indenture made this first day of December in the year of Our Lord One Thousand Eight hundred and thirty nine between David C Taylor and Margarett S his wife of the County of Richmond and State of Virginia of the One part and Severn Mister Sen.r of the County of Northumberland and State aforesaid of the other part Witnesseth. That the said David C Taylor and Margarett S his wife, for and in Consideration of the Sum of Twelve Thousand Dollars Current Money of the United States to them in hand paid and Secured to be paid at and before the Sealing & delivery of these presents by the said Severn Mister Sen.r the receipt Whereof is hereby acknowledged. Have Given, Granted, bargained and Sold enfeoffed conveyed released and Confirmed And by these presents do Give, Grant, bargain and Sell enfeoff Convey release and Confirm unto the said Severn Mister Sen.r his heirs and assigns forever All and Singular that messuage tenement tract or parcel of land, situate in the County of Northumberland aforesaid in Hughletts Neck and bounded by the land of James Harding on the West On the South by the land of Thomas Hughlett, on the east by the Chesapeak Bay and on the North by the land of Thomas Harding and Containing by estimation about Five hundred and fifty acres be the same More or less, for the tract is Sold for Such Quantity little or much, as it Contains which Said tract of land was purchased by the Said David C Taylor from William Harding as by the Deed from the said Harding to the Said Taylor of record in the Clerks Office of the County Court of Northumberland aforesaid will more fully and at large appear; Together with the buildings

This page and following: Deed of sale marking the transfer of the Salt Pond from David C. Taylor to Severn Mister on December 1, 1839. Northumberland County, Virginia, Chancery Causes, *Captain Severn Mister v. David C. Taylor*, 1850-002, Local Government Records Collection, Northumberland Court Records. *Courtesy of the Library of Virginia.*

improvements rights priviledges appurtenances and
Other hereditaments to the same belonging or in any
Manner appertaining And the remainders reversions
rents issues and profits thereof and all the right
title interest and estate of them the said David C
Taylor and Margarett I his wife in and to the same.
To Have and to hold the said Messuage tract or
parcel of land and premises with the appurtenances
unto him the said Severn Mister Senr his heirs and
assigns forever; to his and their sole use benefit and
behoof forever. And the said David C Taylor for
himself his heirs executors and administrators by
these presents Covenants promised and agrees to and
with the said Severn Mister Senr his heirs and assigns
in the following Manner. to wit; that he the said
David C Taylor and his heirs shall and will Warrant
and forever defend the said Messuage tract or parcel
of land and premises with the appurtenances hereby
bargained and sold unto him the said Severn Mister
Senr his heirs and assigns from and against him the
said David C Taylor his heirs and assigns and all
persons Claiming or who may Claim by under or through
him them or any of them and from and against all
Manner of persons and Claims Whatsoever; and further
that he the said David C Taylor and his heirs shall
and will at any time (or at all times) hereafter at
the request and at the costs of him the said Severn
Mister Senr his heirs and assigns Make and execute
any and every Other deed or assurance in the Law for
the more sure and effectual Conveyance of the said
land and premises with the Appurtenances to the said
Severn Mister Senr his heirs and assigns that the
said Severn Mister Senr his heirs and assigns or his
or their Counsel learned in the Law shall or may

devise, advise or require. In Testimony whereof the said David C Taylor and Margarett S his Wife have hereunto Set their hands and affixed their Seals the day and year first above Written.

Signed Sealed and delivered
in presence of –

David C Taylor [Seal]

Margaret S Taylor [Seal]

Richmond County to Wit.

We Benj. D Rust and Fred Lemoine Justices of the peace in the County aforesaid in the State of Virginia do hereby certify that Margarett S Taylor the wife of David C Taylor parties to a certain deed bearing date 1st day of December 1839 and hereto annexed, personally appeared before us in Our County aforesaid, And being examined by us privily and apart from her husband and having the Deed aforesaid fully explained to her, she the said Margaret S Taylor Acknowledged the same to be her act and deed and declared that she had willingly Signed Sealed and delivered the same and that she wished not to retract it. Given under Our hands and seals this 7th day of January 1840

Benj D Rust [Seal]

F. Lemoine [Seal]

of record in the Clerks Office of the County Court of Northumberland aforesaid will more fully and at large appear; Together with the buildings improvement rights priviledges appurtenances and other hereditaments to the same belonging or in any manner appertaining, And the Remanded Reversion Rents issued and the profits thereof and all of the right title interest and the estate of theirs the said David C Taylor and Margarett S his wife in and to the same.

To Have and to hold the said messuage tract or parcel of land and premises with the appurtenances unto him the said Severn Mister Sen'. his heirs and assigns forever, to his and their sole use benefit and behalf forever. And the said David C Taylor for himself his heirs, executors and administrators by these present Covenants promised agreed to and with the said Severn Mister his heirs and assigns in the following manner. To Wit: that he the said David C Taylor and his heirs Shall and will Warrant and forever defend the said Messuage tract or parcel of land and promises with the appurtenances hereby bargained and sold unto him the said Severn Mister and his heirs and assigns from and against him the said David C Taylor his heirs and assigns and all persons Claiming or who may Claim by under or through him these or any of them and from and against all manner of persons and claims Whatsoever; and further that he the said David C Taylor and his heirs shall and will at any time (or at all times) hereafter at the request and at the costs of him the said Severn Mister Send his heirs and assigns. Make and execute any and every Other deed or assurances in the Law for the more sure effectual Conveyance of the said Land and premises with the appurtenances to the said Severn Mister. His heirs and his assigns, that the said Severn Mister his heirs or assigns or his or their counsel learned in the Law shall or only decree advise or require. In Testimony Whereof the said David C and Margarett S his wife have hereunto have set their hands and Affixed their seals the day and year first above mentioned.

Sign Sealed and delivered David C Taylor
In presence of Margaret S Taylor

Richmond County to Wit.

We Benjn D Rush and F Lemoine Justices of the peace in the County aforesaid in the State of Virginia do hereby Certify that Margarett S Taylor the wife of David C Taylor parties to a certain deed bearing date

1ˢᵗ day of December 1839 and hereto amended personally appeared to us in One County aforesaid, and being examined by us privily and apart from her husband and having the Deed aforesaid fully explained to her she the said Margarett S Taylor Acknowledged the Same to be her act and deed and declared that she had Willingly signed sealed and delivered the same and that she wished not to retract it. Given under Our hands and seals this 7ᵗʰ day of January 1840

Benj. D Rush
F. Lemoine

DESCENDANTS OF MARMADUKE MISTER

Author's note: The citations for Appendix D are found in Appendix E and not in the book's Notes section.

GENERATION 1

1. Marmaduke Mister was born around 1660 and he died in approximately 1725. He was the father to William Mister.
   2.   i. William Mister married Patience Harris and died in May of 1744.[1-3]

GENERATION 2

2. William Mister married Patience Harris, the daughter of Jeremiah Harrison. According to the census of 1723, William resided in Somerset County, Maryland, and his estate was probated on May 28., 1744.[1-4] William Mister and Patience Harris had the following children:
   3.   i.   Abraham Mister married Alice, whose last name is not known.[2, 5]
   4.   ii.   William M. Abraham Mister was born in 1720 in Somerset County and married Comfort Evans on October 16, 1749. She was the daughter of John Evans and Arrabella

Turnall. William died February 23, 1807, in Dorchester County, Maryland.[2-3, 5-7]

5. iii. Marmaduke Mister was born in 1722 on Smith Island, Somerset County. He married Rachel between 1758 and 1761, and he later married Sarah between 1770 and 1775. Sarah was born in November 1744. Marmaduke died around April 1798 on Deal Island, Somerset County. His wife, Sarah, died on January 7, 1834, also on Deal Island.[2-3, 5, 8-10]

iv. Judah Mister. (It is not clear if Judah was a male or female, and it could even be possible that this was the Judith Mister that married Richard Evans, but more research is needed).[2]

v. Sarah Mister.[2]

6. vi. Hannah Mister married John Evans on August 21, 1745. John was the son of John Evans and Arrabella Turnall. John was born about 1722 and he died around 1809. [2-3, 11-14]

vii. Sinah Mister.[2]

viii. Patience Mister married a man by the last name of Harper, yet his first name is not known.[2]

GENERATION 3

3. Abraham Mister married Alice. Abraham provided military service to the American forces during the Revolutionary War. On May 12, 1778, Governor Johnson ordered the Maryland Council to pay a sum of 133 pounds to be given to him for sailing his vessel in order to transport colonial troops on at least five separate occasions. [2,5,15] Abraham Mister and his wife had the following child:

i. Stephen C. Mister served as a Loyalist privateer until 1779. In August 1780 he was arrested in Accomack County, Virginia, for treason and piracy and was transported to Richmond. He paid a fine and was to appear in court in October.[9, 16-20]

4. William M. Abraham Mister was born in 1720 in Somerset County, Maryland. On October 16, 1749, he married Comfort Evans, who was the daughter of John Evans and Arrabella Turnall. Mister died on February 23, 1807, in Dorchester County, Maryland.[2-3, 5-7] The couple had the following children:

7.   i.   William Mister was born about 1754 and he married Abigail, who was born around 1757. He died before November 29, 1824. [21]

      ii.   Isaac Mister.[21]

5. Marmaduke Mister was born in 1722 on Smith Island, Somerset County. He married his first wife, Rachel, between 1758 and 1761 and later married Sarah between 1770 and 1775. Sarah was born in November 1744 and died on January 7, 1834, at the age of ninety on Deal Island in Somerset County. In 1783, Mister owned a one-hundred-acre property known as Pitchcraft located on Smith Island south and across from the Little Annemessex River delta. Early in the Revolutionary War, he was mostly known for being a Tory privateer in cahoots with his nephew Captain Stephen Mister and Captain Joseph Wheland. Marmaduke Mister enlisted in the Maryland Militia on August 19, 1780, as a private in the Somerset County, Princess Anne Battalion, Little Annemessex Company, commanded by Colonel Thomas Hayward and Captain Henry Miles. This change in loyalty coincided with the arrest of his privateer nephew, Stephen Mister, in August 1780. His services were still used in a naval capacity by transporting American prisoners back home from the British base in Tangier as listed in the Journal and Correspondence of the State Council of Maryland on May 9, 1782. He signed his will on October 10, 1796, in Somerset County, and he died in April 1798 on Deal Island.[2-3, 5, 8-10, 17, 22-29] Marmaduke Mister and Rachel had the following children:

8.   i.   Sarah Mister was born on June 2, 1761, in Coventry Parish of Somerset County at a place known as Orchard Ridge. Sarah married Solomon Evans, who was the son of Richard Evans and Judith Mister, in 1789 in Accomack County, Virginia. Solomon was born on October 23, 1760. Sarah died on September 12, 1845, and her husband died on December 14, 1852. [3, 30-32]

      ii.   Naomy Mister was born on January 13, 1765, also in Coventry Parish, Somerset County.[31]

9.   iii.   Charity Mister was born on October 24, 1767, on Smith Island, Somerset County and married William Thomas.[31]

      iv.   Elizabeth Betsey Mister was born on September 17, 1770, in Coventry Parish.[31]

Sarah was buried in 1834 on Deal Island, Somerset County, Maryland at the Severn Mister Property, which was also known as The Two Sisters and The Bradshaw House.[10] Marmaduke Mister and Sarah had the following children:

    v.   William Mister was born between 1770 and 1775.[10]

10. vi. Severn Reid Mister was born in 1785 on Smith Island. On July 2, 1805, in Accomack County, he married Keziah C. Evans, the daughter of Richard and Euphemia Evans. Severn died on December 30, 1855, in Talbot County, Maryland.[3, 9-10, 33-34]

6.   Hannah Mister married John Evans, who was the son of John Evans and Arrabella Turnall, on August 21, 1745.[2-3, 11-14] John and Hannah Evans had the following children:

11. i.   Levin Evans was born on February 27, 1744, and he married Mary Byrd on November 7, 1767. Levin died after 1780.[3, 35]

12. ii. Nathan Evans was born on May 10, 1745.[3, 36] He married a woman named Rachel whose last name is not known.

    iii. John Evans was born on December 3, 1747.[3, 37]

    iv. Abigail Evans was born on November 23, 1751.[3, 38]

13. v.   Euphemia "Huffany" Evans was born on September 2, 1754. She married Thomas Evans, the son of Thomas Evans. He was born about 1745 and died around 1794 on Smith Island, Somerset County.[3, 39]

    vi. William Mister Evans was born on October 4, 1757, and he served as a private in the military according to the 1780 enlistment of the Maryland Militia of Somerset County, Princess Anne Battalion, Little Annemessex Company, commanded by Colonel Thomas Hayward and Captain Henry Miles.[3, 22, 40]

14. vii. Jesse Evans was born on July 20, 1761, in Coventry Parish in Somerset County, Maryland, and he married Nancy Evans. She was born on August 15, 1762, and she died on October 27, 1831. Jesse died on February 2, 1835.[3, 12, 41-43]

    viii. Triphenia Evans was born on June 21, 1763.[3, 45]

    ix. Patience Evans was born on April 15, 1765.[3, 46]

GENERATION 4

7. William Mister was born about 1754 and married Abagail. He signed his will on August 30, 1811, in Accomack County, Virginia, and died before November 29, 1824.[21] William Mister and Abigail had the following children:

    i.   Azariah Mister was born about 1786 and died before 1811.[21] He married a woman by the name of Martha Duet.

    ii. Stephen Mister.[21] According to William Mister's will of August 30, 1811, Stephen was estranged from the family and was not residing in Accomack County.

    iii. Jessee Mister.[21] Jessee was also estranged from the family, and according to William Mister's will of August 30, 1811, his whereabouts were unknown.

    iv. William Mister.

8. Sarah Mister was born on June 2, 1761, in Coventry Parish, Somerset County, Maryland at the location known as Orchard Ridge. She married Solomon Evans, the son of Richard Evans and Judith Mister, in 1789 in Accomack County. Solomon was born on October 23, 1760, and died on December 14, 1852. Solomon Evans was a well-known resident of the region and was often referred to as King Solomon. He was buried at the North End Cemetery, Corinth United Methodist Episcopal Churchyard, Ewell, Somerset County. Sarah died on September 12, 1845, and was buried in the Old Churchyard "O'er the Gut" at Orchard Ridge, where she had been born.[3, 30- 32] Solomon Evans and Sarah Mister had the following children:

    i.   Denard Evans was born about 1790, and he died on Deal Island. On December 27, 1807, he married Hannah Evans. She was the daughter of Elijah Thomas Evans and Lovey Evans. She was born about 1797.[3, 53]

    ii. Mitchell Evans was born on September 14, 1792, on Smith Island in Somerset County. He first married a woman whose name is unknown and later married Margaret Peggy Tyler, daughter of John Tyler and Euphemia "Fanny."[3, 55] She was born on October 17, 1811, in Virginia. Margaret died on April 17, 1878, and was buried at the North End Cemetery, Corinth United Methodist Episcopal Churchyard, Ewell.

Mitchell Evans died on February 23, 1857, and was also buried at the North End Cemetery.[3, 54-58]

iii. Elsey Evans was born about 1793. He married Rachel Evans on January 12, 1813, who was born around 1794. He later married Elizabeth Webster on August 13, 1839.[3, 59-60]

9. Charity Mister was born on October 24, 1767, on Smith Island.[31] She married William Thomas, and they had the following child:

   i. Mahala Thomas was born in 1796 on Smith Island. She married Ephraim Tyler. He was born on May 10, 1796, in Tylerton, Somerset County. Ephraim died on May 20, 1844, in Rhodes Point, Somerset County, and he died on March 25, 1879, on Smith Island.

10. Severn Reid Mister was born in 1785 on Smith Island. He married Keziah C. Evans, daughter of Richard Evans and Euphemia, on July 2, 1805, in Accomack County. He owned the Severn Mister Property on Deal Island.[34] This is thought to be the oldest surviving dwelling on Deal Island. Severn Reid Mister later moved to a property in Northumberland County, Virginia, called the Salt Pond. He died on December 30, 1855, in Talbot County, Maryland.[3, 9-10, 33-34] Severn and Keziah had the following children:

   i. Hannah Daniels Mister[3, 61]

   ii. Bennett Mister was born about 1807. He first married Britannia Parks and then later married Mary Daniel in 1838. Bennett Mister was given the Severn Mister Property on Deal Island in November 1839. He died about 1849.[3, 34, 62]

   iii. Richard Mister died on March 13, 1843, in Somerset County. He was buried by the Reverend Vaughan Smith in 1843 on Deal Island at the Severn Mister Property. His cause of death was drowning.[9]

   iv. Lowder Mister was born in 1822. He died on March 13, 1843, in Somerset County. Mister was also buried by the Reverend Vaughan Smith in 1843 on Deal Island at the Severn Mister Property. His cause of death was drowning.[9]

   v. David Mister was born on July 3, 1823. He died on March 13, 1843, in Somerset County. He was buried by the Reverend Vaughan Smith in 1843 at the Severn Mister Property. His cause of death was drowning, the same fate that befell his two elder brothers. [9]

11. Levin Evans was born on February 27, 1744. He married Mary Byrd on November 7, 1767. In 1780, Levin Evans served as a private with the Maryland Militia in the Somerset County, Princess Anne Battalion, Little Annemessex Company, commanded by Colonel Thomas Hayward and Captain Henry Miles during the Revolutionary War.[3, 22, 35, 63] Levin Evans and Mary Byrd had the following children:

    i.   Mary Davis Evans was born on September 10, 1768.[3, 64]

    ii.   John Evans was born on January 10, 1771.[3, 65]

12. Nathan Evans was born on May 10, 1745, and he married Rachel.[3, 36] Nathan and Rachel Evans had the following child:

    i.   Elijah Thomas Evans was born on April 23, 1763. He married Lovey Evans, the daughter of Solomon and Nancy Evans. Lovey was born about 1801 and died on April 25, 1842, in Rhodes Point, Somerset County. Elijah died on June 30, 1841, in Rhodes Point.[3, 66]

13. Euphemia "Hufanny" Evans was born on September 2, 1754, and she married Thomas Evans, the son of Thomas Evans. He was born about 1745 and died around 1794 on Smith Island.[3, 39] Thomas Evans died intestate (meaning without a will). Thomas Evans and Euphemia "Hufanny" Evans had the following children:

    i.   Thomas Evans died about 1822.[3, 67]

    ii.   Mary Polly Evans married Zachariah Crockett, son of Joseph Crockett and a woman with the last name Tyler. He was born about 1765 and died around 1844 in Accomack County, Virginia.[3, 69]

    iii.   Tobias Evans[3, 70]

    iv.   Alcey Evans[3, 71]

    v.   John Evans[3, 72]

    vi.   Euphemia Evans married Thomas Evans.[3, 73]

    vii.   Hannah Evans married William Linton.[3, 74]

    viii.   Josiah Evans was born about 1770.[3, 75]

    ix.   Rachel Evans was born around 1775 and she married Richard Dickey Evans, son of Richard Evans and Mary Molly Crockett. He was born about 1770. Richard died on Tangier Island, Accomack County. Rachel died around 1865 on Tangier Island as well.[3, 76]

    x.   Peter Evans was born about 1790. He married Zipporah Evans, daughter of Thomas Evans, on June 16, 1808.

Zipporah was born approximately 1797 and died on October 9, 1855. He married Maria Handy on December 22, 1835. His second wife was born about 1800. Peter died in September 1858.[3, 68]

xi. Hezekiah Evans was born around 1794, and he married Sally Evans on May 19, 1812.[3, 77]

14. Jesse Evans was born on July 20, 1761, in Coventry Parish, Somerset County. He married Nancy Evans, who was born on August 15, 1762, and died on October 27, 1831. In 1780, Jesse Evans also served as a private with the Maryland Militia in the Princess Anne Battalion, Little Annemessex Company, 23rd Regiment of Somerset County. Nancy Evans was buried in Ewell, Somerset County. Jesse signed his will in December 1832 in Somerset County, and he died on February 2, 1835, and was buried in Ewell as well.[3, 12, 22, 41-44, 78-79] Jesse Evans and Nancy Evans had the following children:

i. Delitha Evans[3, 80]

ii. William Evans was born about 1786 in Rhodes Point, Somerset County. He married Ann Evans, who was born around 1790 also in Rhodes Point. William died about 1835.[3, 81]

iii. Laban Evans was born on August 29, 1789. He married Elizabeth Tyler, daughter of Thomas Tyler, on December 26, 1812, who was born approximately in 1791. Later, he married Sally Parks, daughter of Job Parks and Rachel Crockett, on July 16, 1819. She died on November 19, 1869. His third marriage was to Mary Ann Jones on August 28, 1838; she was born around 1809 at Mount Vernon and she died about 1889. Laban Evans died on November 19, 1869, and was buried in Ewell.[3, 42, 82-83]

iv. Benjamin Moss Evans was born on January 14, 1791, and married Charity Evans, daughter of Solomon Evans, who was born on October 10, 1801. He died on August 15, 1864, in Ewell. Benjamin was buried in the North End Cemetery, Corinth United Methodist Episcopal Churchyard, Ewell. His wife died in Ewell on March 29, 1864, and was buried in the same cemetery.[3, 84]

v. Rachel B. Evans was born on August 27, 1796, and died on August 15, 1852. She married William Evans on August 11, 1819, in Somerset County. William was born about

1798, the son of Richard Evans and Euphemia Evans. He followed her in death around 1856. Rachel B. Evans was buried in Ewell.[3, 42, 85-86]

vi. Alihu Evans was born approximately 1799, and he married Rhoda Bradshaw, daughter of Richard Bradshaw and Arrabella Mister, who was born around 1806. Alihu eventually died about 1842.[3, 87-88]

vii. Noah Evans was born on March 5, 1807, on Smith Island. He married Patience Mister, who was the daughter of Azariah Mister and Martha Duet, on July 25, 1832, in Somerset County. Noah died on Smith Island on July 11, 1845, and was buried in the North End Cemetery, Corinth United Methodist Episcopal Churchyard, Ewell.[3, 43, 47-51] Patience was born about 1811 in Rhodes Point, Somerset County, and she died much later than her husband on January 26, 1893, on Smith Island.

viii. Polly Todd Evans was born on April 12, 1807. She married Severn Bradshaw, son of Jacob Bradshaw and Levenia Evans. He was born about 1807 and he died in approximately 1889. Polly died on July 6, 1890.[3, 42, 89-91]

SOURCES FOR APPENDIX D

1. Brøderbund Software, Inc., World Family Tree Vol. 2, Ed. 1 (Name: Release date: November 29, 1995), Tree No. 1794. Date of Import: January 29, 1999.
2. Maryland Prerogative Court (MD), William Mister Will, Vols. 23–24, 1743–1746.
3. Brøderbund, Tree No. 1794.
4. Ancestry.com, Maryland, Compiled Census and Census Substitutes Index, 1772–1890 (Provo, UT).
5. Somerset County Deeds (Somerset County, MD), Vol. 24: 127, June 17, 1762.
6. Brøderbund, Tree No. 1794.
7. Browne, William Hand, Maryland State Archives (Baltimore, MD, Friedenwald Company, Maryland Historical Society, 1893), Journal and Correspondence of the Council 1778–1779 Volume 21, p. 76.
8. Brøderbund, Tree No. 1794.
9. Wallace, Adam, *The Parson of the Islands: a Biography of the Rev. Joshua Thomas* (Philadelphia, PA, Author; Collins, printer; William W. Harding, stereotyper, 1861).
10. Somerset County Will Book (Somerset County, MD), EB17 pp. 665–666.
11. Brøderbund, Tree No. 1794.
12. Ancestry.com, Maryland, Births and Christenings Index, 1662–1911 (Provo, UT, USA, Ancestry.com Operations, Inc., 2011), Ancestry.com, Record for Jesse Evens. http://search.ancestry.com/cgi-bin/sse.dll?db=FSMarylandBirth&h=70800&indiv=try.
13. Ancestry.com, Maryland, Marriages, 1634–1777 (Provo, UT, USA, Ancestry.com Operations, Inc., 2012), Ancestry.com, Record for Hannah

Mister. http://search.ancestry.com/cgi-bin/sse.dll?db=MDmarriages&h=15386&indiv=try.

14. Yates Publishing, U.S. and International Marriage Records, 1560–1900 (Provo, UT, USA, Ancestry.com Operations Inc, 2004), Ancestry.com, Source number: 1244.208; Source type: Family group sheet, FGSE, listed as parents; Number of Pages: 1. Record for Hannah Mister. http://search.ancestry.com/cgi-bin/sse.dll?db=WorldMarr_ga&h=843906&indiv=try.

15. Journal and Correspondence of the Council of Maryland (Annapolis, MD, Maryland State Archives, 1778–1779), p. 76.

16. Walczyk, Gail M, Walczyk, Gail M (Coram, NY, Petersrow), *Tangier in the American Revolution*. https://www.petersrow.com/main/bay_islands/tangier_1.htm.

17. Shomette, Donald G, *Pirates on the Chesapeake* (Centreville, MD, Tidewater Publishers, 1985).

18. Eller, Ernest McNeill, *Chesapeake Bay in the American Revolution* (Centreville, MD, Tidewater Publishers, 1981), p. 392.

19. Boyd, Julian P., *The Papers of Thomas Jefferson* (Princeton, NJ, Princeton University Press, 1951), Volume 3, 1951.

20. Journal and Correspondence of the Council of Maryland (October 27 1779–November 11, 1780), August 3, 1780.

21. Accomack County Wills (Accomack County, VA,), William Mister's Will. 1824–1825: 271. August 30, 1811.

22. Maryland Militia Muster Rolls, Maryland Historical Society, Special Collections Archivist Maryland Historical Society, 201 West Monument Street Baltimore, Maryland 21201.

23. Maryland Indexes (Assessment of 1783), p. 124.

24. Force, Peter, *American Archives: a Documentary History of the United States of America* (Washington, M. St. Clair Clarke and Peter Force, April 1848), Fifth Series, Vol. 1, p. 687.

25. Browne, William Hand, Maryland State Archives (Baltimore, MD, Friedenwald Company, Maryland Historical Society, 1893), Journal and Correspondence of the Maryland Council of Safety, July 7–December 31, 1776. Pp. 152–156. Mariman's Deposition, July 27, 1776; Yell's Deposition, July 27, 1776.

26. Browne, William Hand, Maryland State Archives (Baltimore, MD, Friedenwald Company, Maryland Historical Society, 1893), Journal and Correspondence of the Council of Maryland, 1778–1779, p. 333. C.C p. 229. Council to Grayson, In Council Annapolis March 30, 1779.

27. Browne, William Hand, Maryland State Archives (Baltimore, MD, Friedenwald Company, Maryland Historical Society, 1893), Journal and

Correspondence of the State Council of Maryland. November 19, 1781–November 14, 1782. p. 160. May 9. Liber C.B. No. 24 p. 274. Marmaduke Mister has permission to return home by the 15 (May), he having brought some American prisoners from Tangier Island.

28. Naval Documents of the American Revolution (Washington, DC, United States Government Printing Office, 1970), Vol. 15, American Theatre: May 9, 1776–July 31, 1776, Part 6 of 8, pp. 1247–1248. July 27, 1776.

29. Browne, William Hand, Maryland State Archives (Baltimore, MD, Friedenwald Company, Maryland Historical Society, 1893), Journal and Correspondence of the State Council of Maryland. November 19, 1781–November 14, 1782. p. 160. May 9. Liber C.B. No. 24 p. 274.

30. Brøderbund, Tree No. 1794.

31. Ancestry.com, Maryland, Births and Christenings Index, 1662–1911 (Provo, UT, USA, Ancestry.com Operations, Inc., 2011), Ancestry.com, FHL Film Number: 14417.

32. Brøderbund, Tree No. 1794.

33. Ibid.

34. Maryland Historical Trust, Bradshaw House (https://mht.maryland.gov/secure/medusa/PDF/Somerset/S-46.pdf,), Bradshaw House / Two Sisters. https://mht.maryland.gov/secure/medusa/PDF/Somerset/S-46.pdf.

35. Brøderbund, Tree No. 1794.

36. Ibid.

37. Ibid.

38. Ibid.

39. Ibid.

40. Ibid.

41. Ibid.

42. Ancestry.com, U.S., Find A Grave Index, 1600s–Current (Provo, UT, USA, Ancestry.com Operations, Inc., 2012), Ancestry.com, Record for Jesse Evans. http://search.ancestry.com/cgi-bin/sse.dll?db=FindAGrave US&h=45229007&indiv=try.

43. Ancestry.com, U.S., Find A Grave Index, 1600s–Current (Provo, UT, USA, Ancestry.com Operations, Inc., 2012), Ancestry.com, Record for Noah Evans. http://search.ancestry.com/cgi-bin/sse.dll?db=FindAGrav eUS&h=45229055&indiv=try.

44. Wright, F Edward, Maryland Eastern Shore Vital Records, p. 83.

45. Brøderbund, Tree No. 1794.

46. Ibid.

47. Ibid.

48. Dodd, Jordan, Liahona Research, comp., Maryland Marriages, 1655–1850 (Provo, UT, USA, Ancestry.com Operations Inc, 2004), Ancestry.com, Record for Patience Minter. http://search.ancestry.com/cgi-bin/sse.dll?db=MDmarriages_ga&h=158882&indiv=try.

49. Ancestry.com, U.S., Find A Grave Index, 1600s–Current (Provo, UT, USA, Ancestry.com Operations, Inc., 2012), Ancestry.com, Record for Patience Tyler. http://search.ancestry.com/cgi-bin/sse.dll?db=FindAGraveUS&h=99064108&indiv=try.

50. Ancestry.com, 1850 United States Federal Census (Provo, UT, USA, Ancestry.com Operations, Inc., 2009), Ancestry.com, Year: 1850; Census Place: Dames Quarter, Somerset, Maryland; Roll: M432_297; Page: 456B; Image: 219. Record for Patience Tylor. http://search.ancestry.com/cgi-bin/sse.dll?db=1850usfedcenancestry&h=17898352&indiv=try.

51. Ancestry.com and The Church of Jesus Christ of Latter-day Saints, 1880 United States Federal Census (Provo, UT, USA, Ancestry.com Operations Inc, 2010), Ancestry.com, Year: 1880; Census Place: Smith Island, Somerset, Maryland; Roll: 515; Family History Film: 1254515; Page: 376D; Enumeration District: 074; Image: 0400. Record for Patience Tyler. http://search.ancestry.com/cgi-bin/sse.dll?db=1880usfedcen&h=35680042&indiv=try.

52. Brøderbund, Tree No. 1794.

53. Ibid.

54. Arthur Rich Cullen, cullen.FTW (Name:rich@cullen.net), http://rich.cullen.net/, Date of Import: May 28, 1999.

55. Brøderbund, Tree No. 1794.

56. Arthur Rich Cullen, cullen.FTW (Name:rich@cullen.net), http://rich.cullen.net/, Date of Import: May 28, 1999.

57. Brøderbund, Tree No. 1794.

58. Arthur Rich Cullen, cullen.FTW (Name:rich@cullen.net), http://rich.cullen.net/, Date of Import: May 28, 1999.

59. Brøderbund, Tree No. 1794.

60. Ibid.

61. Ibid.

62. Ibid.

63. Maryland Militia Muster Rolls, Maryland Historical Society, Special Collections Archivist Maryland Historical Society, 201 West Monument Street Baltimore, Maryland 21201.

64. Brøderbund, Tree No. 1794.

65. Ibid.

66. Ibid.

67. Ibid.

68. Ibid.

69. Ibid.

70. Ibid.

71. Ibid.

72. Ibid.

73. Ibid.

74. Ibid.

75. Ibid.

76. Ibid.

77. Ibid.

78. Clements, S. Eugene and Wright, F. Edward, *The Maryland Militia in the Revolutionary War* (Rear 63 East Main Street, Westminster, MD 21157, Family Line Publications, 1987), Library of Congress, p. 221.

79. Princess Anne Courthouse, Somerset County, Maryland Wills 1820–37.

80. Brøderbund, Tree No. 1794.

81. Ibid.

82. Ibid.

83. Ibid.

84. Ibid.

85. Ibid.

86. Ibid.

87. Dodd, Jordan, Liahona Research, comp., Maryland Marriages, 1655–1850 (Provo, UT, USA, Ancestry.com Operations Inc, 2004), Ancestry.com, Record for Rachel Evans. http://search.ancestry.com/cgi-bin/sse.dll?db=MDmarriages_ga&h=71238&indiv=try.

88. Brøderbund, Tree No. 1794.

89. Ibid.

90. Ibid.

91. Ancestry.com and The Church of Jesus Christ of Latter-day Saints, 1880 United States Federal Census (Provo, UT, USA, Ancestry.com Operations Inc, 2010), Ancestry.com, Year: 1880; Census Place: Smith Island, Somerset, Maryland; Roll: 515; Family History Film: 1254515; Page: 374D; Enumeration District: 074; Image: 0396. Record for Pollie Bradshaw. http://search.ancestry.com/cgi-bin/sse.dll?db=1880usfedcen&h=49459461&indiv=try.

NOTES

Introduction

1. Ernest McNeill Eller, *Chesapeake Bay in the American Revolution* (Centreville, MD: Tidewater, 1981), 378.
2. Barry Paige Neville, "For God, King, and Country: Loyalism on the Eastern Shore of Maryland During the American Revolution," *International Social Science Review* 84, no. 3/4 (2009): 135.
3. Eller, *Chesapeake Bay*, 69.
4. Ibid.
5. Ibid.
6. Alan Flanders, "Andrew Sprowle's Widow Lost it All, Including Her Good Name," *The Virginian-Pilot* (Norfolk), February 10, 2002.
7. Frances W. Dize, *Smith Island, Chesapeake Bay* (Centreville, MD: Tidewater Publishers, 1990), 53.
8. Eller, *Chesapeake Bay*, 204.
9. Ibid., 395.
10. Charles Henry Lincoln, *Naval Records of the American Revolution 1775–1788* (Washington, D.C.: Government Printing Office, 1906): 3.
11. S. Eugene Clements and F. Edward Wright, *The Maryland Militia in the Revolutionary War* (Westminster, MD: Family Line Publications, 1987), 35.
12. Lincoln, *Naval Records*, 3.
13. Neville, "For God, King, and Country," 149.
14. Eller, *Chesapeake Bay*, 244.

15. Ibid., 243.
16. Lindsey Gruson, "Changes Sweeping Chesapeake Bay Threaten and [*sic*] Island's Old Way of Life," *New York Times*, June 15, 1986.
17. Dize, *Smith Island*, 37.
18. Clements and Wright, *Maryland Militia*, 221.

Part One

19. Neville, "For God, King, and Country," 136.
20. Eller, *Chesapeake Bay*, 379.
21. Neville, "For God, King, and Country," 136.
22. Ibid., 137.
23. Ibid.
24. Ibid.
25. Eller, *Chesapeake Bay*, 379.
26. Ibid., 381.
27. Neville, "For God, King, and Country," 146.
28. Ibid.
29. Ibid., 147.
30. Eller, *Chesapeake Bay*, 383.
31. William Hand Browne, *Journal and Correspondence of the Maryland Council of Safety*, July 7–December 31, 1776 (Baltimore, MD: Maryland Historical Society, 1893): 350.
32. Eller, *Chesapeake Bay*, 384.
33. Clements and Wright, *Maryland Militia*, 35–36.
34. *Journal and Correspondence of the State Council of Maryland*, November 19, 1781–November 14, 1782: 362.
35. Ibid.
36. Charles J. Truitt, *Breadbasket of the Revolution, Delmarva's Eight Turbulent War Years* (Salisbury, MD: Historical Books, Inc., 1975), 141.
37. Clements and Wright, *Maryland Militia*, 35.
38. *Journal*, November 19, 1781–November 14, 1782, 363.
39. Neville, "For God, King, and Country," 139.
40. Ibid.
41. Ibid., 141.
42. Ibid.
43. Ibid.
44. Ibid., 143.

45. Ibid., 144.
46. Freeborn Garrettson, accessed July 12, 2018, https://www.francisasburytriptych.com/book-series/characters/freeborn-garrettson/.
47. Neville, "For God, King, and Country," 143.
48. Ibid.
49. Garrettson.
50. Eller, *Chesapeake Bay*, 385.
51. Ibid., 398–399.
52. Ibid., 387.
53. Ibid.
54. Ibid.
55. Neville, "For God, King, and Country," 136.

Part Two

56. Ibid., 146.
57. Dize, *Smith Island*, 40.
58. Ibid.
59. William Hand Browne, *Journal and Correspondence of the Maryland Council of Safety*, January 1–March 20, 1777, *Journal and Correspondence of the State Council*, March 20, 1777–March 28, 1778 (Baltimore, MD: Maryland Historical Society, 1897): 164.
60. Ibid., 189–190.
61. Keith Mason, "Localism, Evangelicalism, and Loyalism: The Sources of Discontent in the Revolutionary Chesapeake," *The Journal of Southern History* 56, no. 1 (February 1990): doi:10.2307/2210663.
62. Neville, "For God, King, and Country," 148.
63. Ibid., 149.
64. Mason, "Localism, Evangelicalism, and Loyalism."
65. Neville, "For God, King, and Country," 147.
66. Ibid.
67. Ibid., 145.
68. Charles R. Lampman, "Privateers of the Revolution," *SAR Magazine* 106, no. 4 (Spring 2011): 21.
69. Ibid., 22.

Part Three

70. Neville, "For God, King, and Country," 146.

71. Donald G. Shomette, *Pirates on the Chesapeake: Being a True History of Pirates, Picaroons, and Raiders on Chesapeake Bay, 1610–1807* (Centreville, MD: Tidewater Publishers, 1985), 256.

72. Dize, *Smith Island*, 41.

73. Shomette, *Pirates on the Chesapeake*, 256.

74. Eller, *Chesapeake Bay*, 382.

75. Ibid.

76. Shomette, *Pirates on the Chesapeake*, 256.

77. Ibid., 257.

78. Ibid.

79. Eller, *Chesapeake Bay*, 381.

80. Shomette, *Pirates on the Chesapeake*, 257.

81. Dize, *Smith Island*, 41.

82. Shomette, *Pirates on the Chesapeake*, 258.

83. Ibid.

84. Browne, *Journal*, July 7–December 31, 1776, 152–155.

85. Ibid., 155–156.

86. Shomette, *Pirates on the Chesapeake*, 258–259.

87. Eller, *Chesapeake Bay*, 382.

88. Peter Force, *American Archives: Containing a Documentary History of the United States of America, From the Declaration of Independence, July 4, 1776, to the Definite Treaty of Peace with Great Britain, September 3, 1783*, vol. 1, series 5 (Washington, DC: M. St. Clair Clarke and Peter Force, April, 1848), 686.

89. Browne, *Journal*, July 7–December 31, 1776, 407–408.

90. Dize, *Smith Island*, 42.

91. Shomette, *Pirates on the Chesapeake*, 260.

92. Ibid.

93. Ibid., 260–261.

94. Ibid., 265.

95. Ibid., 266.

96. Eller, *Chesapeake Bay*, 393.

97. Shomette, *Pirates on the Chesapeake*, 267.

98. Ibid., 283.

99. Eller, *Chesapeake Bay*, 389.

100. Ibid.

101. Ibid., 390.

102. Ibid.

103. Ibid.

104. Ibid., 391.

105. Isaac J. Greenwood, "Cruising on the Chesapeake in 1781," *Maryland Historical Magazine* 5, no. 2 (June 1910).

106. Dize, *Smith Island*, 51.

107. Eller, *Chesapeake Bay*, 394.

108. Woodrow T. Wilson, *History of Crisfield and Surrounding Areas on Maryland's Eastern Shore* (Baltimore, MD: Gateway Press, 1974), 246–247.

Part Four

109. Eller, *Chesapeake Bay*, 234.

110. Ibid., 386.

111. *Journal and Correspondence of the Council of Maryland*, January 1–December 31, 1781: 584–585.

112. Eller, *Chesapeake Bay*, 234.

113. Ibid., 235.

114. Ibid., 235–236.

115. Shomette, *Pirates on the Chesapeake*, 271.

116. T.W. White, "The Virginia Navy of the Revolution, Part III," *Southern Literary Messenger; Devoted to Every Department of Literature and the Fine Arts* 24, no. 3 (March 1857): 216, accessed September 26, 2017, http://quod.lib.umich.edu/m/moajrnl/acf2679.0024.003/220: 216.

117. Eller, *Chesapeake Bay*, 235.

118. Ibid.

119. Dize, *Smith Island*, 45.

120. Randy Stuart, "Why you shouldn't cross a man like General John Cropper, Jr.," History Between the Waters, May 14, 2014, accessed September 14, 2017, http://esvhs.blogspot.com/2014/05/why-you-shouldnt-cross-man-like-general.html.

121. Thomas J. Rogers, *A New American Biographical Dictionary: Or Remembrancer of the Departed Heroes, Sages, and Statesmen of America. Confined Exclusively to Those who Signalized Themselves in Either Capacity, In the Revolutionary War which obtained the Independence of their country; with Important Alterations and Additions*, 3rd ed. (Easton, PA: Thomas J. Rogers, 1824), 168.

122. Joab Trout, "A Revolutionary Relic. A Sermon Preached on the Eve of the Battle of Brandywine, Sept. 10, 1777 by the Reverend Joan Trout"

(speech, Battle of Brandywine, Delaware County, PA), accessed January 27, 2019, http://lccn.loc.gov/15008362.

123. Rogers, *A New American Biographical Dictionary*, 168.

124. Barton Haxall Wise, "Memoir of General John Cropper," in *Proceedings of the Virginia Historical Society at the Annual Meeting Held December 21–22, 1891, with Historical Papers Read on the Occasion, and Others*, vol. XI (Richmond, VA: Virginia Historical Society, 1892), 283.

125. Ibid.

126. Ibid.

127. Ibid.

128. Ibid.

129. Ibid., 295.

130. Stuart, "Why you shouldn't.".

131. Wise, "Memoir of General John Cropper," 284.

132. Ibid., 286.

133. Stuart, "Why you shouldn't.".

134. Wise, "Memoir of General John Cropper," 287.

135. Ibid.

136. Ibid., 291.

137. Stuart, "Why you shouldn't.".

Part Five

138. Eller, *Chesapeake Bay*, 239.

139. Shomette, *Pirates on the Chesapeake*, 290.

140. Eller, *Chesapeake Bay*, 240.

141. Ibid.

142. Shomette, *Pirates on the Chesapeake*, 290.

143. Eller, *Chesapeake Bay*, 241.

144. Bill Helin, "The Battle of the Barges," History Between the Waters, March 26, 2014, accessed September 14, 2017, http://esvhs.blogspot.com/2014/03/the-battle-of-barges.html.

145. Eller, *Chesapeake Bay*, 242.

146. Ibid.

147. Rogers, *A New American*, 168.

148. White, "The Virginia Navy," 216.

149. Eller, *Chesapeake Bay*, 242.

150. Ibid., 243.

151. Helin, "Battle of the Barges.".

152. Eller, *Chesapeake Bay*, 243.

153. Ibid.

154. White, "The Virginia Navy," 217.

155. Eller, *Chesapeake Bay*, 243.

156. Rogers, *A New American*, 169.

157. Eller, *Chesapeake Bay*, 244.

158. Ibid.

159. Bud Hannings, *Chronology of the American Revolution: Military and Political Actions Day by Day* (Jefferson, NC: McFarland & Company, Inc., 2008), 490.

160. Hank Burchard, "Digging Up a Few Good Pirates," *Washington Post*, May 13, 1988.

161. Gardner Weld Allen, *A Naval History of the American Revolution*, vol. 2 (Boston, MA: Houghton Mifflin, 1913), 597.

162. White, "The Virginia Navy," 219.

163. Ibid., 217.

164. Rogers, *A New American*, 169.

165. Wise, "Memoir of General John Cropper," 300.

166. Ibid.

167. White, "The Virginia Navy," 220.

168. Ibid., 217.

169. Ibid., 218.

170. Eller, *Chesapeake Bay*, 244.

171. Wise, "Memoir of General John Cropper," 301.

172. White, "The Virginia Navy," 217.

173. Helin, "Battle of the Barges.".

174. Eller, *Chesapeake Bay*, 244.

175. Shomette, *Pirates on the Chesapeake*, 298.

176. Dize, *Smith Island*, 47.

177. Shomette, *Pirates on the Chesapeake*, 299.

178. Helin, "Battle of the Barges.".

179. History.com Staff. "Treaty of Paris." History.com. 2009. Accessed September 26, 2017. http://www.history.com/topics/american-revolution/treay-of-paris.

180. Eller, *Chesapeake Bay*, 245.

Part Six

181. Harold Hancock, *The History of Nineteenth Century Laurel* (Westerville, OH: Otterbein College Print Shop), 1.

182. John Fitzhugh Millar, *Buccaneers Davis, Wafer & Hingson, and the Ship Batchelors Delight*, report, William and Mary, 2010, accessed July 31, 2018, htttp://50th.wm.edu/1967/Bachelors_Delight.pdf.

183. Hancock, *Nineteenth Century Laurel*, 2.

184. Millar, *Buccaneers Davis, Wafer & Hingson*.

185. Ibid.

186. Hancock, *Nineteenth Century Laurel*, 2.

187. *Journal and Correspondence of the Council of Maryland*, 1778–1779: 76.

188. Somerset County Deeds, June 17, 1762, Vol. 24: 127.

189. Examination of Reuben Warrington for aiding Stephen Mister to break jail (Accomack County Court September 16, 1777) (Virginia Center for Digital History, Alderman Library, Dist. file).

190. Stephen Mister, escapes prison (Accomack County Court) (Virginia Center for Digital History, Alderman Library, Dist. file).

191. *Journal and Correspondence of the Council of Maryland*, 1778–1779: 333.

192. Trial of Stephen Mister, May 1780 (Accomack County Court) (Virginia Center for Digital History, Alderman Library, Dist. file).

193. *Journal and Correspondence of the Council of Maryland*, October 27, 1779–November 11, 1780: 247.

194. Julian P. Boyd, *The Papers of Thomas Jefferson*, vol. 3, June 18, 1779, to September 30, 1780 (Princeton, NJ: Princeton University Press, 1951).

195. Clements and Wright, *Maryland Militia*, 221.

196. *Journal and Correspondence of the Council of Maryland*, July 1–December 31, 1780: 489.

197. *Journal and Correspondence of the State Council of Maryland*, November 19, 1781–November 14, 1782: 160.

198. Dize, *Smith Island*, 51.

199. Maryland State Archives, *1783 Tax Assessment Somerset County Maryland*, 124, http://msa.maryland.gov/msa/stagser/s1400/s1437/html1437so.html.

200. Virginia Commission on Boundary Lines (1870–1874), *Report and Accompanying Documents of the Virginia Commissioners Appointed to Ascertain the Boundary Line Between Maryland and Virginia* (Richmond, VA: R.F. Walker, Superintendent Public Printing, 1873), 203.

201. Somerset County, MD, Somerset County Will Book, EB17 (Annapolis, MD: Maryland State Archives, 1796): 665–666.

Part Seven

202. Paul Touart, *Maryland Historical Trust Determination of Eligibility Form*, June 19, 1986, Somerset County Historical Trust, Princess Anne.
203. Dize, *Smith Island*, 53.
204. Ibid., 57.
205. Ibid.
206. Ibid., 61.
207. John C. Fredriksen, John C. *America's Military Adversaries: From Colonial Times to the Present* (Santa Barbara, CA: ABC-CLIO, 2001), 116.
208. Adam Wallace, *The Parson of the Islands: a Biography of the Rev. Joshua Thomas: Embracing Sketches of His Contemporaries: and Remarkable Camp Meeting Scenes, Revival Incidents, and the Reminiscences of the Introduction of Methodism on the Islands of the Chesapeake and Eastern Shores of Maryland and Virginia* (Baltimore, MD: Thomas and Evans Printing Company, 1906), 238.
209. Dize, *Smith Island*, 111.
210. Wallace, *The Parson of the Islands*, 282.

Part Eight

211. Carroll W. Adams, "The History of the Ownership of Salt Pond Farm," *The Bulletin of the Northumberland County Historical Society* 111, no. 1 (July 1966): 25.
212. Paul Touart, *Maryland Historical Trust Determination of Eligibility Form*, June 19, 1986, Somerset County Historical Trust, Princess Anne.
213. Northumberland County, VA, Chancery Causes, Capt. Severn Mister v. David C Taylor, 1850-002, Local Government Records Collection, Northumberland Court Records (Richmond, VA: The Library of Virginia).
214. Ibid.
215. Wallace, *The Parson of the Islands*, 298.
216. Ibid., 300.
217. Ibid., 301.
218. David M. Ludlum, *The Early American Winters, II: 1821–1870* (Boston, MA: American Meteorological Society, 1968), 43.
219. John W. Nielsen and Brent McRoberts, "March 1843: The Most Abnormal Month Ever?" in *Historical Climate Variability and Impacts in North America* (Dordrecht: Springer).

220. Wallace, *The Parson of the Islands*, 301–302.

221. Ibid., 303.

222. Northumberland County, VA, Chancery Causes, Capt. Severn Mister v. David C Taylor, 1850-002, Local Government Records Collection, Northumberland Court Records (Richmond, VA: The Library of Virginia).

223. Ibid.

224. Wallace, *The Parson of the Islands*, 303.

225. Ibid., 305.

226. Dize, *Smith Island*, 66.

Conclusion

227. Eller, *Chesapeake Bay*, 386.

228. William Hand Browne, *Journal and Correspondence of the Maryland Council of Safety*, January 1–March 20, 1777, *Journal and Correspondence of the Maryland State Council*, March 20, 1777–March 29, 1778 (Baltimore, MD: Maryland Historical Society, 1897): 176.

229. Eller, *Chesapeake Bay*, 400.

230. Ibid., 391.

231. Neville, "For God, King, and Country," 135.

232. Eller, *Chesapeake Bay*, 393.

233. Wise, "Memoir of General John Cropper," 303.

234. Dize, *Smith Island*, 44.

Appendix A

235. Wise, "Memoir of General John Cropper," 299.

236. Lincoln, *Naval Records*, 87.

237. Ibid., 271.

BIBLIOGRAPHY

Adams, Carroll W. "The History of the Ownership of Salt Pond Farm." *The Bulletin of the Northumberland County Historical Society* 111, no. 1 (July 1966): 21–28.

Allen, Gardner Weld. *A Naval History of the American Revolution.* Vol. 2. Boston, MA: Houghton Mifflin, 1913.

Babits, Lawrence C. "Using the Principles of War Archaeology for a Better Understanding for Behavior on the Battlefield." Edited by Dana Lee Pertermann and Holly Kathryn Norton. In *The Archaeology of Engagement: Conflict and Resolution in the United States*, 74–94. Texas A&M University, 2015.

"Bowman's Folly, Accomack County." Accessed May 26, 2018. Division of Historic Research. http://www.dhr.virginia.gov/registers/Counties/Accomack/nr_bowmans_folly_photos.htm.

Boyd, Julian P. *The Papers of Thomas Jefferson.* Vol. 3. June 18, 1779, to September 30, 1780. Princeton, NJ: Princeton University Press, 1951.

Browne, William Hand. *Journal and Correspondence of the Maryland Council of Safety.* July 7–December 31, 1776. Baltimore, MD: Maryland Historical Society, 1893.

———. *Journal and Correspondence of the Maryland Council of Safety.* January 1– March 20, 1777, *Journal and Correspondence of the State Council.* January 1–March 28, 1778. Baltimore, MD: Maryland Historical Society, 1897.

Burchard, Hank. "Digging Up a Few Good Pirates." *Washington Post*, May 13, 1988.

Clements, S. Eugene, and F. Edward Wright. *The Maryland Militia in the Revolutionary War*. Westminster, MD: Family Line Publications, 1987.

Cronin, William B. *The Disappearing Islands of the Chesapeake*. Baltimore and London: The John Hopkins University Press, 2005.

Dize, Frances W. *Smith Island, Chesapeake Bay*. Centreville, MD: Tidewater Publishers, 1990.

Eller, Ernest McNeill. *Chesapeake Bay in the American Revolution*. Centreville, MD: Tidewater Publishers, 1981.

Esnauts, and Rapilly. "*Carte de la partie de la Virginie ou l'armée combinée de France & des États-Unis de l'Amérique a fait prisonnière l'Armée anglaise commandée par Lord Cornwallis le 19 octobre. 1781, avec le plan de l'attaque d'York-town & de Glocester*." Map. Paris, 1781.

Examination of Reuben Warrington for aiding Stephen Mister to break jail (Accomack County Court September 16, 1777) (Virginia Center for Digital History, Alderman Library, Dist. file).

Flanders, Alan. "Andrew Sprowle's Widow Lost it All, Including Her Good Name." *Virginian-Pilot* (Norfolk), February 10, 2002.

Force, Peter. *American Archives: Containing a Documentary History of the United States of America, From the Declaration of Independence, July 4, 1776, to the Definite Treaty of Peace with Great Britain, September 3, 1783*. Vol. 1. Series 5. Washington, D.C.: M. St. Clair Clarke and Peter Force, April 1848.

Fredriksen, John C. *America's Military Adversaries: From Colonial Times to the Present*. Santa Barbara, CA: ABC-CLIO, 2001.

"Freeborn Garrettson." The Asbury Triptych Series. Accessed July 12, 2018. https://www.francisasburytriptych.com/book-series/characters/freeborn-garrettson.

Gainsborough, Thomas. *Charles Cornwallis, 1st Marquess Cornwallis*. 1783. National Portrait Gallery, London, England.

Greenwood, Isaac J. "Cruising on the Chesapeake in 1781." *Maryland Historical Magazine* 5, no. 2 (June 1910): 123–31.

Gruson, Lindsey. "Changes Sweeping Chesapeake Bay Threaten and [*sic*] Island's Old Way of Life." *New York Times*, June 15, 1986.

Hall, Henry Bryan. *Thomas Nelson, Jr.* 1870.

Halls, John James. *Portrait of Cockburn*. 1817. National Maritime Museum, Greenwhich, London.

Hancock, Harold. *The History of Nineteenth Century Laurel*. Westerville, OH: Otterbein College Print Shop, 1983.

Hannings, Bud. *Chronology of the American Revolution: Military and Political Actions Day by Day*. Jefferson, NC: McFarland & Company, Inc., 2008.

Helin, Bill. "The Battle of the Barges." History Between the Waters. March 26, 2014. Accessed September 14, 2017. http://esvhs.blogspot.com/2014/03/the-battle-of-barges.html.

History.com Staff. "Treaty of Paris." History.com. 2009. Accessed September 26, 2017. http://www.history.com/topics/american-revolution/treay-of-paris.

Journal and Correspondence of the Council of Maryland. 1778–1779.

———. October 27, 1779–November 11, 1780.

———. July 1–December 31, 1780.

———. January 1–December 31, 1781.

Journal and Correspondence of the State Council of Maryland. November 19, 1781–November 14, 1782.

Lampman, Charles R. "Privateers of the Revolution." *SAR Magazine* 106, no. 4 (Spring 2011): 18–23.

Lincoln, Charles Henry. *Naval Records of the American Revolution 1775–1788.* Washington, D.C.: Government Printing Office, 1906.

Ludlum, David M. *The Early American Winters, II: 1821–1870.* Boston, MA: American Meteorological Society, 1968.

MacKubin, Florence. *Sir Robert Eden.* 1914. Maryland State Archives, Annapolis, MD.

Maryland State Archives. *1783 Tax Assessment Somerset County Maryland.* 124. http://msa.maryland.gov/msa/stagser/s1400/s1437/html/1437so.html. MSA S 1437.

———. *Somerset County, Maryland Wills 1820–37.* Princess Anne, MD: Princess Anne Courthouse, 1837, 241–42.

Mason, Keith. "Localism, Evangelicalism, and Loyalism: The Sources of Discontent in the Revolutionary Chesapeake." *The Journal of Southern History* 56, no. 1 (February 1990): 23–54. doi:10.2307/2210663.

Millar, John Fitzhugh. *Buccaneers Davis, Wafer & Hingson, and the Ship Batchelors Delight.* Report. William and Mary. 2010. Accessed July 31, 2018. htttp://50th.wm.edu/1967/Bachelors_Delight.pdf.

Naval Documents of the American Revolution; American Theatre: May 9, 1776–July 31, 1776. Vol. 5. Series 6. Washington, D.C.: United States Government Printing Office, 1970. Electronically Published by American Naval Records Society, Bolton Landing, NY, 2012.

Neville, Barry Paige. "For God, King, and Country: Loyalism on the Eastern Shore of Maryland During the American Revolution." *International Social Science Review* 84, no. 3/4 (2009): 135–56. Accessed December 3, 2016. http://www.jstor.org/stable/41887408.

Nielsen, John W., and Brent McRoberts. "March 1843: The Most Abnormal Month Ever?" In *Historical Climate Variability and Impacts in North America*, 123–45. Dordrecht: Springer.

Northumberland County, VA, Chancery Causes. Capt. Severn Mister v. David C Taylor, 1850-002. Local Government Records Collection, Northumberland Court Records. The Library of Virginia. Richmond, VA.

Peale, Charles Willson. *Portrait of General Cropper*. 1793. Catalog of American Portraits, Smithsonian Institute, Washington, D.C.

———. *Portrait of William Paca*. 1822. Maryland State Archives, Annapolis, MD.

———. *Thomas Johnson*. 1824. Maryland State Archives, Annapolis, MD.

———. *William Smallwood, 1732–1792 from life*. 1781–1782. Maryland State Archives, Annapolis, MD.

Reynolds, Joshua. *Portrait of John Murray, 4th Earl of Dunmore (1730–1809)*. 1765. Scottish National Gallery, Edinburgh, Scotland.

Rogers, Thomas J. *A New American Biographical Dictionary: Or, Rememberancer of the Departed Heroes, Sages, and Statesmen, of America ; Confined Exclusively to Those who Have Signalized Themselves in Either Capacity, in the Revolutionary War ; with Important Alterations and Additions*. 3rd ed. Easton, PA: Thomas J Rogers, 1824.

Rosenthal, Albert. *Luther Martin*. 1905. Legal Portrait Collection, Harvard Law School Library, Cambridge, MA.

Shomette, Donald G. *Pirates on the Chesapeake: being a true history of pirates, picaroons, and raiders on Chesapeake Bay, 1610–1807*. Centreville, MD: Tidewater Publishers, 1985.

Somerset County Deeds. June 17, 1762. Vol. 24: 127.

Somerset County, Maryland Wills. Vol EB 17. Annapolis, MD: Maryland State Archives, 1796.

Stephen Mister, escapes prison (Accomack County Court) (Virginia Center for Digital History, Alderman Library, Dist. file).

Stuart, Gilbert. *Bishop William White*. C. 1795. Pennsylvania Academy of Fine Arts, Philadelphia, PA.

Stuart, Randy. "Why you shouldn't cross a man like General John Cropper, Jr." History Between the Waters. May 14, 2014. Accessed September 14, 2017. http://esvhs.blogspot.com/2014/05/why-you-shouldnt-cross-man-like-general.html.

Tho. Jefferson to Governour Lee. August 15, 1780. In *Letters Relating to North America, 1775, 1780. Ff. 1–34*. British Library, Add MS 38650 A.

Thomson, J. *Freeborn Garrettson.* United Methodist General Commission on Archives and History, Madison, NJ.

Touart, Paul. *Maryland Historical Trust Determination of Eligibility Form.* June 19, 1986. Somerset County Historical Trust, Princess Anne, MD.

Trial of Stephen Mister (Accomack County Court May 6, 1780) (Virginia Center for Digital History, Alderman Library, Dist. file).

Trout, Joab. "A Revolutionary Relic. A Sermon Preached on the Eve of the Battle of Brandywine, Sept. 10, 1777 by the Reverend Joab Trout." Speech, Battle of Brandywine, Delaware County, PA. Accessed January 27, 2019. http://lccn.loc.gov/15008362.

Truitt, Charles J. *Breadbasket of the Revolution, Delmarva's Eight Turbulent War Years.* Salisbury, MD: Historical Books, Inc., 1975.

Trumbull, John. *Surrender of Lord Cornwallis.* 1820. Rotunda, United States Capitol, Washington, D.C.

Virginia Commission on Boundary Lines (1870–1874). *Report and Accompanying Documents of the Virginia Commissioners Appointed to Ascertain the Boundary Line Between Maryland and Virginia.* Richmond, VA: R.F. Walker, Superintendent Public Printing, 1873.

Wallace, Adam. *The Parson of the Islands: a Biography of the Rev. Joshua Thomas: Embracing Sketches of His Contemporaries: and Remarkable Camp Meeting Scenes, Revival Incidents, and the Reminiscences of the Introduction of Methodism on the Islands of the Chesapeake and Eastern Shores of Maryland and Virginia.* Philadelphia, PA: Adam Wallace, 1861.

Ward, Harry M. *For Virginia and for Independence: Twenty-Eight Revolutionary War Soldiers from the Old Dominion.* Jefferson, NC: McFarland & Company, Inc., 2011.

White, T. W. "The Virginia Navy of the Revolution, Part III." *Southern literary messenger; devoted to every department of literature and the fine arts* 24, no. 3 (March 1857): 210–21. Accessed September 26, 2017. http://quod.lib.umich.edu/m/moajrnl/acf2679.0024.003/220.

Wilson, Woodrow T. *History of Crisfield and Surrounding Areas on Maryland's Eastern Shore.* Baltimore, MD: Gateway Press, 1974.

Wise, Barton Haxall. "Memoir of General John Cropper." In *Proceedings of the Virginia Historical Society at the Annual Meeting Held December 21–22, 1891, with Historical Papers Read on the Occasion, and Others,* 273–316. Vol. XI. Richmond, VA: Virginia Historical Society, 1892.

Wright, F. Edward. *Maryland Eastern Shore Vital Records 1751–1775.* Westminster, MD: Family Line Publications, 1984.

INDEX

ABOUT THE AUTHOR

eonard Szaltis attended St. Ambrose University in Davenport, Iowa, where he studied history and earned a B.A. and a B.M.E. He later studied business and earned an MBA from St. Ambrose University. He continued his graduate coursework at Boston University and earned an M.M. in education. The author has taught history and business in public schools in Iowa and Illinois. He is also an active member of the Sons of the American Revolution.

Visit us at
www.historypress.com